MONEY
THE PERSONAL FINANCE AND PROPERTY VALUE COLLECTION

JORDAN PARKER
GERALD R. WALTON

© Copyright 2019 - All rights reserved.

The content contained within this book may not be reproduced, duplicated or transmitted without direct written permission from the author or the publisher.

Under no circumstances will any blame or legal responsibility be held against the publisher, or author, for any damages, reparation, or monetary loss due to the information contained within this book, either directly or indirectly.

Legal Notice:

This book is copyright protected. It is only for personal use. You cannot amend, distribute, sell, use, quote or paraphrase any part, or the content within this book, without the consent of the author or publisher.

Disclaimer Notice:

Please note the information contained within this document is for educational and entertainment purposes only. All effort has been executed to present accurate, up to date, reliable, complete information. No warranties of any kind are declared or implied. Readers acknowledge that the author is not engaging in the rendering of legal, financial, medical or professional advice. The content within this book has been derived from various sources. Please consult a licensed professional before attempting any techniques outlined in this book.

By reading this document, the reader agrees that under no circumstances is the author responsible for any losses, direct or indirect, that are incurred as a result of the use of information contained within this document, including, but not limited to, errors, omissions, or inaccuracies.

❦ Created with Vellum

INTRODUCTION

You can think about financial freedom as building a house that you are planning to live in for the rest of your life. You cannot build a beautiful and comfortable home without a strong foundation. In terms of financial freedom, the foundation is personal financial management. This includes budgeting and improving your credit score. Starting a business and increasing your wealth are the house that you build upon it.

Some people think that financial freedom is all about how the house looks — the paint job, the furniture, the lavish decor. However, if the foundation was not built properly, the house will collapse sooner or later, no matter how beautiful it is. Before starting construction on the house, you first need to make sure that your foundation is level and structurally sound. In other words, if you can master your budget and credit score, you will be able to build your wealth and run a successful business as a result.

Changing the way you handle your resources is a fundamental process. Your behavior towards spending, saving, and managing money will have a significant effect on your decision-making processes when you delve into business ventures that are meant to multiply your wealth. This is what we will discuss in the first chapter, Mastering Budgeting and Credit Score to Your Advantage, which will guide you through effective methods for laying the foundation for sustainable personal financial management.

Word of warning, this book will not tell you what to do with your finances because there is not a specific 12-step program to changing your current financial habits. Instead, I will present you with different techniques and methods that I truly believe can help you build a better relationship with money. From budgeting techniques to methods in paying and avoiding debt to dealing with spending-related guilt, all of these can change your attitude towards money. However, I understand that readers of this book have different financial situations and goals. It will be up to you to decide which of these techniques will help you establish a good foundation that is key to achieving financial freedom.

The second chapter, Build Wealth and Run a Successful Business without Leaving Your Family Life Aside, is about growth. To be exact, I will take you through different processes that are meant to make better use of your resources. I will also teach you different methods on how you can make your finances grow both actively and passively. The aim of this chapter is to enable you to experience financial freedom in a more holistic way. That means finding a balance between different money-making avenues and your personal, social, and family lives.

At the end of the second chapter, my hope is that you find a new drive to make your finances grow. Consequently, I also want you to learn how to find common ground between your relationship with money and your relationship with the most important people in your life. Believe it or not, it is possible to excel in both of these areas at the same time.

With research and data from financial experts, combined with my knowledge and mastery as a financial mentor, your overall attitude towards money will change after reading this book. Are you ready to build skills that will lead to financial stability and freedom? Let's get started.

MASTERING BUDGETING AND CREDIT SCORE TO YOUR ADVANTAGE

As I mentioned in the introduction, this chapter of the book deals with the foundation of financial freedom. You need to be able to master you budget and credit score, so you will have stable underlying financial habits that guide you through all of your financial decisions.

In this chapter, you will learn about different budgeting types, what will work best for you, and how you can stick to a budget that you set for yourself. We will also discuss the psychology of debt and how you can change the most-common spending habits that put people into debt. Moreover, I will introduce you to the minimalist lifestyle and how it can help you save money that you can put towards your superior financial goals. Lastly, we will talk about spending-related guilt and how you can avoid it.

At the end of this chapter, you will find some helpful tips from experts on how you can master budgeting. These tips have helped me in my own personal journey to financial freedom, and I think they can also be useful in your pursuit of your financial goals.

But before any of that, let's begin the discussion and dive into the basics of budgeting.

DIFFERENT BUDGETING TYPES: WHICH ONES DO WORK AND WHICH DON'T

There are four common types of budgeting for personal use: the time-based budget, the cash-only budget, the barebones budget, and the irregular-income budget. I have personally tried these budgeting types at some point in my life and I can confidently say that they are all effective in managing your finances. However, not all methods will always work for everybody. To help you determine what budgeting type suits your situation, consider the following:

- Do you have a regular income?
- How much do you earn in a week, a month, or a year?
- What are your basic necessities?
- Do you have recurring expenses that you do not consider as necessities?
- Are there any big occasions coming up that you need to spend on?

Take a moment to answer these questions. Create a spreadsheet or write it down on a piece of paper. In one column, list every item that you consider a necessity. In another column, jot down every recurring expense that you can live without. Lastly, look at the year ahead and think of any special events that are lined up.

Here's a pro tip for you: When making a list of your expenses, you need to learn to distinguish between what you want and what you need. You also have to consider the urgency of the items on your list. You will use these variables to determine which expenses you need to prioritize. To be exact, here is the order in which you should allocate your resources:

1. High-priority (HP) expenses are items that are both important and urgent. These include food, transportation, and other daily needs.
2. Mid-priority (MP1) expenses are items that are important but not urgent, like your bills that are due in the future. However, as their due date comes closer, these expenses will move from MP1 to HP. At the same time, items that are urgent but not important also belong in this category (MP2). Examples of these expenses are going out on a Friday night or attending a concert. As a rule of thumb, try to minimize urgent, but not important expenses, so you do not end up breaking your budget plan.
3. Low-priority (LP) expenses are items that are neither important nor urgent. These include shopping for new clothes, redecorating your home, or buying the latest smartphone even though your current device still works properly.

Categorizing your expenses in terms of importance and urgency will prevent you from running out of resources or getting into debt. Always use this system in assessing your resource allocation.

In addition, you should also consider saving a fixed percentage of your savings. Say you plan to put 20% of your monthly income into your savings account before you pay off any bills. Doing so will help you avoid the risk of spending what could be your savings on MP2 and LP items.

Are you done answering the questions? Great! Let's now discuss the different budgeting types and find which one will work for you.

. . .

Time-based Budget

When you plan your budget on a yearly, monthly, or weekly basis, you have a time-based budget plan. This method of personal financial planning makes a note of the most important things that you need and when you need to pay them. It also gives you a bird's-eye view of how you spend your money over a given period of time. Because you know where your resources are going, it can help you manage them better and move them around when you need to, especially when there are unforeseen costs like a personal or medical emergency. A yearly or monthly budget plan will also take into account any events that you may need to spend on such as a birthday party, a wedding, or a holiday.

What time-based budget plan should you use?

From experience, most people use a monthly budget plan. The reason for this is that utilities and other bills are usually due on a monthly basis, and a monthly budget plan enables you to keep track of expenses that are both important and urgent.

Although it is the most common, a monthly budget plan also has its downsides. It is not as broad as a yearly budget plan, so you cannot plan for big events that are coming within the year. It is also not as detailed as a weekly budget plan, so you do not have a clear picture of your day-to-day expenses.

The solution: Create two or more time-based budget plans at the same time. It is actually advisable to do this because it will enable you to manage and track your spending in a more comprehensive way.

How do you make a time-based budget plan?

Let's say that you are creating a monthly budget plan. To

start off, the first thing you need to do is to identify your income sources. Create an income table and list all of your sources of income in one column. This includes your monthly paycheck after taxes, cash flow that comes from side gigs and other ventures, stipends or grants if any, etc. Indicate how much you earn from each source on the next column. Then, sum up your income and put the total in bold text on the last row of the amount column.

Next, you need to create a table for your expenses. Look back at the list you made earlier and begin to input all HP and MP1 expenses. These include your rent, utilities, and other bills like insurance, social security contributions, student loan payments, etc. For items that are necessities but do not have a fixed amount, such as food and transportation, you can set a monthly allowance to spend. If you are paying off a debt, it should appear in this section too.

After these items, input MP2 expenses and other miscellaneous items such as subscriptions for Netflix, Hulu, Spotify, etc. Then, just like the income table, sum up your expenses and put the total in bold text on the last row of the amount column.

The final step is to subtract your expenses from your income to see how much is left for unforeseen costs and things that you want but do not necessarily need. During this step, you can also decide to cut back on certain expenses, beginning with the LP items, when your budget is a little tight.

If you are up to it, you can find out how much of your monthly income is taken by each expense subcategory. You can do this by dividing an expense by your monthly income. For example, if your food budget is $250 and your income is $2,000, then food takes up 12.5% of your monthly budget. This is a deeper analysis of your monthly spending which will give you an insight into your spending habits.

. . .

Should you use a time-based budget plan?

A time-based budget plan may not work for people with irregular income sources (see irregular-income budget) because this type of budgeting assumes that you have a steady cash flow when you plan your finances for a certain time period. Otherwise, this is a basic budget planning method that you can easily implement and stick to in the long run. It is also highly customizable; you can be as detailed and as analytical as you like.

Cash-only Budget

When you implement a cash-only budget, you pay any and all expenses with cash (or a debit card for certain transactions). This personal financial planning method enables you to drastically change your spending behavior by limiting the amount of money you are allowed to spend. More importantly, it will help those who are trying to gain control of their finances and to create healthier spending habits.

Aside from these benefits, a cash-only budget plan allows you to prioritize. Because you are working with a limited budget, you are forced to set aside cash for HP and MP1 expenses first. Therefore, you are able to pay bills on time and pay debts sooner. You also avoid spending money on things you do not need.

What do you need for a cash-only budget plan?

Beyond the HP, MP1, MP2, and LP expense categories, you need to create more specific classifications for your expenses. Here is an example:

- HP expenses: Food, groceries, transportation (commute or gas)
- MP1 expenses: Water, electricity, internet bill,

phone bill, social security contribution, student loan payment
- MP2 expenses: Netflix, Spotify, Friday drinks
- LP expenses: None

Create these subcategories before you proceed to the next section. To help you stick to a cash-only budget plan, you will also need several envelopes or pouches to put cash in.

How do you make a cash-only budget plan?

For the purposes of this example, let's say that you are creating a cash-only budget plan for the month ahead.

Unlike the time-based budget plan, the first thing you consider when making a cash-only budget plan is your expenses. How much are you spending for each subcategory? In total, how much are you expecting to spend this month? (Remember: The answer should not be more than your total monthly income and should not eat into your savings.) This is the amount you will be withdrawing from your account. You can withdraw a little over your expected total expense for emergencies (consider these additional dollars your "rainy day fund"), but you are only allowed to spend this much for the whole month. You are not allowed to use your credit card. As much as possible, you should also avoid using a debit card unless you really have to.

Now get your envelopes or pouches; they should be as numerous as your expense subcategories. Label each envelope according to your subcategories, and then divide your cash allowance for the month into these envelopes. You can use different colors of pens to mark each envelope for how urgent and/or important the item is. For instance, use a red pen for HP and MP1 expenses, a black pen for MP2 expenses, and a blue pen for LP expenses.

The trick with a cash-only budget plan is to stick to the

amount that you decided to put in each subcategory. For instance, when your food envelope is running low, consider staying in and cooking dinner instead of going out. Moreover, a cash-only budget plan also requires you to become a smarter and more conscious spender. When you grab drinks with friends, you would not want to spend all of your "Friday night drinks" budget on one night out, wouldn't you? You stretch your allowance according to your budget.

Should you use a cash-only budget plan?

This is a restrictive budget plan to say the least, and it is designed to be. You can say that it is like quitting cold turkey on your unhealthy spending behavior. Often, a drastic change like this is ineffective for certain habit reformation techniques. But you will be surprised at how easily this budgeting technique can change your whole relationship with money.

However, this budget plan may not be suitable for families, especially those with children. Children come with a lot of unforeseen costs, like school projects or events, which will make it hard to plan your budget in a cash-only basis. It may also not work for people whose jobs involve a lot of traveling. In this case, using a credit card is often more convenient for a lot of transactions.

The good news is you can pair a cash-only budget plan with other budgeting techniques, such as a time-based budget plan. You can set a cash limit on select subcategories and then adjust your monthly budget as you would with a time-based budget plan.

Barebones Budget

If you think a cash-only budget plan is extremely constraining, you clearly have not heard of a barebones budget plan. A barebones budget plan is strictly for HP and MP1 expenses only. In other words, you cannot have MP2 and LP expenses. It cuts off any non-essential costs and allocates your resources only on necessities.

A barebones budget plan is what you enforce when you suddenly lose a job or experience a dire personal or medical emergency. You can also implement it if you are trying to pay off a huge debt in a short period of time.

How do you make a barebones budget plan?

Creating a barebones budget plan is easy. Ask yourself, what are my necessities? What items can I live without? The former is your HP and MP1 expenses, and you will only allocate resources for these items. You can combine a cash-only budget plan with the barebones budget plan, so you are not tempted to withdraw from your account or to use your credit card on MP2 and LP expenses.

Should you use a barebones budget plan?

Yes, but only if you fall under any of the circumstances mentioned above. A barebones budget plan will help those who are working with a limited resource pool for an extended period of time.

However, there is no reason for anyone with a steady source of income and/or practically no debt to implement a barebones budget plan. Consider this budgeting technique your emergency plan.

Irregular-Income Budget

If you are a freelancer, you probably work on commission and therefore have an irregular income, so it is more challenging to implement a consistent budget plan like the first two techniques we discussed. However, there are a few things you can do to make sure that you are not breaking the bank or spending more than what you earn as a freelancer. Here are a few tips for anyone with an irregular income:

- Pay off HP and MP1 expenses as soon as possible, even if the due date for them is still far off.
- Cut back on MP2 and LP expenses as much as you can.
- Set up a contingency plan for when clients fail to pay you on time. (A barebones budget plan will come in handy for this situation.)
- To avoid late payments, include penalties for clients in your freelancing contract. For instance, you can enforce a 2% late payment fee if a client fails to settle an invoice within 10 working days after receiving it. At the same time, you can offer discounts and other perks for clients who always pay on time.

How do you make an irregular-income budget plan?

To create an irregular-income budget plan, you need a list of your HP and MP1 expenses. Set a date to pay all of your regular bills at the same time even if they have different due dates. For food, transportation, and the like, decide on an exact amount that you can spend. Implement a cash-only budget plan mindset for these items, i.e., find a way to efficiently distribute your resources over a given period of time. For instance, if you ever feel tempted to spend a good chunk of your food budget on one fine dining experience, ask yourself whether that is worth the strict budgeting that you will have to enforce afterwards.

Should you use an irregular-income budget plan?

Despite what you may think, an irregular-income budget plan is not only for freelancers. Small business owners will also benefit from this technique, especially at the start of their entrepreneurship journey. At the same time, even those with a regular paycheck can implement an irregular-income budget plan to practice mindfulness in spending.

IS PSYCHOLOGY INVOLVED IN PEOPLE'S DEBT HABITS?

In theory, debt management is simple. Amar, Ariely, Ayal, Cryder, and Rick (2011) explained it in foolproof terms:

...people should first pay the minimum payment for each debt (to avoid surcharges and penalties), and then use all available cash to pay down the loan with the highest interest rate. Once this loan has been paid off, people should move to the loan with the next highest interest rate, and so on.

This strategy prevents any debt from growing while you slowly pay off each of them. It will also be useful in your overall personal financial management because you will have an accurate idea of how much debt you still owe and how you can successfully settle it all.

However, a lot of people still find debt management extremely difficult. In the United Kingdom, the total household debt in 2018 rose to £1,785 billion from £1,735 billion in 2017 (Harari, 2018), which was a £50-billion growth. Meanwhile, the total household debt in the United States rose to $13.5 trillion at the end of 2018, which was a $32-billion increase from just the previous quarter (Heeb, 2019). If debt management is so simple, why aren't people better at it?

The answer can be found in psychology. According to Amar et al. (2011), people are more likely to perceive debt as one big goal that they divide into smaller and more manageable subgoals. This cognitive approach to debt often leads to the pursuit of subgoals instead of managing resources towards the ulterior goal. In addition, people are also more likely to become motivated when a subgoal is achievable, i.e., one is more motivated to pay a certain amount to a smaller debt than to pay a similar amount to a bigger debt because the former is quicker and easier to settle. Lastly, most people are more motivated to reduce their number of debts instead of the total amount of their debt.

For example, say you are currently paying your student loan, credit card bills, and home mortgage. Instead of using the strategy presented earlier, you decide to divide and conquer your debts, i.e., you focus on paying your credit card bills first since they have the smallest balances and therefore will take the quickest time to settle. This sounds like a good idea; once you finish paying your credit card bills, you are left with only two debts to pay.

But while you are paying off your credit card bills, your student loan and home mortgage will grow given their respective interest rates. Before you know it, you are in more debt than you were in the beginning.

Mental health also plays a role in debt management. According to a lecture by Dr. Richardson (2015), there is correlation among one's socioeconomic status, mental health, and debt. In fact, they have a cyclical relationship. They all directly affect each other.

Let me explain. Families in a lower socioeconomic class are more likely to get in more debt than families in a higher socioeconomic class. As a result, a person in a lower socioeconomic class is more likely to develop a mental health issue such as anxiety and depression due to stress over debt and worsening financial status. At the same time, debt can cause mental health issues that will prevent a person from finding a stable job; without a regular income, paying off their debts will become more difficult. Existing mental health conditions also lead people to be in debt. In fact, people with mental health disorders are 16% more likely to be in debt than people without mental health disorders. Among people with mental health disorders, it is 24% more likely to be in debt than to have no debt (Richardson, 2015).

While psychology does play a role in a person's debt habits, there are other factors that affects one's ability to pay off a debt. Ruben (2009) listed some of these factors which include innovations in crediting systems that entice more people to apply for mortgage and other smaller loan agreements. The wider availability of credit also encourages consumers to take advantage. Meanwhile, increasing interest rates hinders one's ability to pay their debt consistently. Of course, socioeconomic factors, such as modest incomes and risk-based pricing against mid-to-low-income families, also have an effect on debt management and may even lead to a poverty debt trap.

Common Debt Habits

Aside from the abovementioned causes of debt, there is an undeniable personal liability when it comes to this financial problem. You have to make some adjustments in how you manage your resources if you want to avoid accumulating debt. Before we discuss your next course of action, let's first identify some common debt habits that you need to change.

Number one, stop following trends. In this current age of social media, a lot of people are influenced to keep up with the latest trends at the risk of their own financial stability. For instance, buying the latest smartphone in the market even though you still have a perfectly functioning gadget at your disposal is a terrible financial decision. In every purchase, ask yourself whether it is practical or just for show.

Number two, stop using shopping as a coping mechanism. As discussed earlier, there might be some underlying mental health issues that are causing you to adopt unhealthy spending behaviors. Like, do you usually spend more money when you are depressed? If so, you have to realize that this will not be a sustainable or a healthy way to deal with your issues in the long run. In fact, debt can cause higher levels of stress and anxiety, which can make your depression worse.

Number three, stop being an impulse buyer. You have to practice mindfulness in every purchase. Whenever you buy something from the store or online, avoid browsing. Just go straight to the product that you need to buy and then check out, so you will not be tempted to add more items to your cart.

By changing these common debt habits, you are one step closer to financial freedom. However, I want to remind you that you cannot change your spending behaviors overnight, and that's okay. During times of temptation, there is one thing I want to reiterate – be mindful how you spend your money. Do not focus on the short-term happiness that a purchase will bring; always think about the long-term effects of your financial decisions.

How can you avoid debt?

To avoid debt, I will give you actionable steps to take. The following course of action can save you from debt before you even acquire it. In the case of existing debt, it will help you to better and more efficiently allocate your resources, so you can reach financial freedom as soon as possible.

First and foremost, do not borrow an amount that is beyond your means to pay. You learned about the time-based budgeting technique earlier. This will actually help you in assessing your ability to pay before you borrow money or apply for a loan. Look at your yearly and monthly budget plans. Is there any room left in your budget? Is it enough to pay installments? If you answered no to one or both of these questions, then do not put yourself into debt, no matter how small. In the case of an emergency, you may not be able to pay an installment, causing your debt to grow.

Second, ask yourself if the debt is necessary. How will you be using what you plan to owe? Will it help you during a personal or a medical crisis? Or is it for an MP2 or an LP expense? If you are risking your financial stability to shop for new clothes or to go on a vacation, I think it is obvious what you must do — stop before you get into debt!

Third, if you are currently finding it difficult to pay off your debts, implement a cash-only budget plan. The last thing you need in this situation is to acquire new debt by using your credit card. By shifting to a cash-only basis for any and all transactions, you will avoid the temptation of making another credit card or online purchase.

Lastly, cut back on MP2 and LP expenses until you find balance in your financial status again. You can even use these items as motivation to pay off your debt. For example, if you have an outstanding credit card balance, you can stop your Netflix subscription, turn down any invitations to a night out, and cook all of your meals at home until you pay it off.

These steps may seem small, but they are steps towards financial freedom nonetheless. The key is persistence. You need to be diligent in following this course of action if you want to see a significant change in your current level of debt.

HOW TO SET A BUDGET AND STICK TO IT

Now that you have a clearer idea of how to create a budget plan that works for you and to manage existing debt without stress, let's talk about sustainability. How do you set a budget and, more importantly, stick to it? In this part of the book, I will teach you 20 hacks for sticking to a budget, beginning with…

1. Never spend money that you don't have.

There is a reason why you listed all of your income sources and that is to have a precise idea of your ability to spend. When you make a budget plan, your expenses cannot exceed your income. At the same time, after making your budget plan, do not make unnecessary purchases that will make your expenses bigger than your income. These tips seem like common sense, but they are still worth mentioning so you can remember.

2. Create a shopping list for food and grocery items.

Think for a second about the way you shop for food and grocery items. Do you always go to the store with a list? On the occasions that you did not bring a shopping list, did you check out with items that you did not originally intend to buy? Most, if not all, people will answer yes to the last question. It may not be the case all of the time, but it often happens. This common mistake leads to more expenses that you have not planned for. When you shop, avoid making this mistake in the first place by creating a shopping list and not buying items that are not on it.

3. Keep your receipts and other transaction records.

Your receipts and other transaction records will give you a pretty good idea of where your money went over a given period of time. If you somehow strayed from your budget plan, it will help you pinpoint problem areas in your spending habits. And even though you managed to stay on track, these will be useful in creating a simple overview of how you spent your money. They can show you exactly how much you spent on HP, MP1, MP2, and LP expenses, as well as subcategories like food, transportation, entertainment, etc.

4. Look for cheaper alternatives whenever you can.

To buy anything for stature, influence, or clout is a big financial blunder. For example, the brand Supreme has become a trendy label that people purchase primarily for social status. A long-sleeved crew neck with the red Supreme box logo retails for more than $1,000. A white shirt with the same logo costs a couple hundred bucks. Why would you spend this much money on a shirt when you can buy clothes that are as comfortable but way more affordable?

Of course, you can splurge once in a while, but it should be well within your means. If you are still paying off a loan or a debt, you are only putting yourself in greater financial hardship by spending money on expensive things. This applies to all purchases, not just designer clothes.

5. Cut costs as much as you can.

If you really try to be mindful of your spending habits, you will find a lot of ways to cut back on your expenses. For example, instead of eating out or getting takeout most of the week, try cooking half your meals at home. By eliminating tips alone, you will save a significant amount of money.

Here is another example. How much does your Starbucks addiction cost in a month? In a year? A $3 venti iced latte once a day will cost $90 a month and $1,080 a year. If you put that money into your savings, you will have $10,800 without interest in 10 years! Do you see how thinking long term can significantly and positively impact your financial stability? Home-brewed coffee sounds more appealing now, doesn't it? Plus, skipping Starbucks will not only help you save money; it will also allow you to become more environmentally responsible because you won't be using plastic straws and cups.

6. Try thrifting.

Thrift stores are a great place to find MP2 and LP items such as clothes, shoes, and bags. Though items here are secondhand, you will still find most of them in good condition and with a significantly lower price tag. Based on experience, you can find products from known brands at up to an 80-90% markdown! There are other items at the thrift store too, like furniture and decor items for your home.

7. Sell items that you do not use anymore.

You can sell old clothes, shoes, bags, books, gadgets, and the like that are still in good condition and then use the money you earn from these items to fund your MP2 and LP expenses. Aside from helping you earn extra cash that you can add to your budget, you will also be able to declutter your living space.

8. Try DIY.

Doing things yourself (DIY) can help you stay within budget for home improvements, repairs, and other projects. You will not have to call a professional and pay their fees if you DIY. If you do not know how to do something, like how to fix a leaking pipe, you can always search the internet for a video tutorial. You can also DIY and eliminate certain expenses like paying for a car wash by cleaning your own car or laundry service by doing your own laundry.

9. Fix broken things before buying brand new.

Some people would prefer to throw out broken things and to buy replacements instead of finding ways to fix them. For example, if you have a few old shirts with holes in them, sew them before you go shopping. Assess whether something can be repaired before you decide to buy brand new. Not only will this help you stay within budget, it will also make you a wiser and more responsible consumer.

10. Save water and electricity.

Your utilities are priority expenses that you cannot completely eliminate from your budget. However, there are ways to minimize their costs. Here are a few examples:

- Switch off lights when not in use.
- Unplug appliances and electronic gadgets when not in use.
- Unplug your laptop and phone chargers when the batteries are full.
- Do not use your TV as background noise.
- Try to avoid using an air conditioner. Buy an electric fan that consumes less power or open the windows to let fresh air in.
- If you must use an air conditioner, keep the door

closed to help regulate the temperature.
- Try to avoid using a hair dryer and/or iron. Wake up a little bit earlier in the day so you can towel or air dry your hair before going to work. Alternatively, shower at night.
- Be mindful of your water consumption.
- If a faucet is leaking, fix it immediately.
- If you have a laundry unit at home, do bigger loads once or twice a week instead of smaller loads several days a week.

These are just some of the things that you can do to reduce your water and electric bills. Although these simple acts may not lead to hundreds of dollars of savings per month, they will still make your expenses more manageable.

11. Cancel your gym membership.

According to the International Health, Racquet & Sportsclub Association (Rodriguez, 2018), the global health club industry was worth $87.2 billion in 2017. In the United States alone, there were a total of 60.9 million memberships and more than 38,000 clubs. At an average monthly cost of $58, an American spends $696 annually for their gym membership (Crockett, 2019).

But why would you work out at the gym when you can jog around your neighborhood or hike on a nearby trail? The outdoors don't cost a cent and won't charge you hidden fees. Therefore, you should consider canceling your gym membership especially if you only go there a few times per month. There are other ways to work out a sweat and maintain physical fitness. Unless you are a regular gym person, there is no reason for you to keep spending $696 per year.

12. If you cannot do the time, do not do the crime.

Are you thinking of spending money on a big purchase that is not on your budget? How long before you can pay off that debt? Thinking about the time it will take to settle an expense will demotivate you from going over budget. Similarly, you can look back and count how many hours of labor it took to earn the money that you plan on spending. Is all the hard work worth this purchase? Probably not, so why buy it?

13. Get a reusable water bottle.

The cost of a bottle of water may not seem like much, but it can really add up if you buy several of them every day. Like getting coffee from Starbucks, you can save money if you bring your own water instead. After all, it is easy to find a place to refill your bottle when you run out of water; you probably have a water station at work or in school. More importantly, you will be able to contribute to protecting our planet by reducing your plastic waste.

14. Cancel duplicate subscriptions.

Subscription payments make it more manageable to afford a service. However, if you are working on a tight budget, paying subscription fees for virtually similar services is not a good financial decision. For example, Netflix and Hulu are both streaming services. Though they have their own content, they are still a redundant entertainment expense. Choose which one you like better or use more often and then cancel the other one.

15. Borrow one-use items.

This hack applies for items that you intend to only use once. For example, if you are attending a wedding, do not bother buying an expensive outfit if you have a friend who can lend you clothes and shoes. Are you planning a camping trip? Ask your colleagues if they have any gear you can borrow. If you do not have a power tool that you need for a project, maybe your dad has what you need. You can postpone and completely prevent unplanned spending by asking others for help.

16. Try meal prepping

Because food is an HP expense, you cannot completely

remove it from your budget. However, there is always something you can do to minimize the amount of money you spend on food. For instance, take cooking at home to the next level by meal prepping.

Meal prepping involves making whole dishes ahead of time. For example, you can cook meals for the coming week in a single day. Store them in the fridge in microwave-safe and airtight containers until you want to eat them. When you already have meals prepared, you have no good reason to spend additional money on food. Here are other financial benefits of meal prepping:

- If you have a family, meal prepping means buying ingredients in bulk, which can lead to discounts.
- You avoid wasting perishable food items by cooking them immediately.
- You do not have to think about where to go to eat, which will help you avoid temptations.
- You can take your prepared meals to work or school, so you do not have to spend money for lunch.
- You know exactly how much you are spending on food.

Aside from these financial benefits, meal prepping will also help you stay on track with your fitness goals. You can plan dishes that are healthy and good for you when you meal prep.

17. Find an accountability partner.

When it comes to exercise, I found that a workout buddy helps me remain motivated. I have more drive to stay fit and to work on my physical fitness when I have a friend to jog, bike, or hike with.

The same sentiment can be applied to forming healthier financial habits. You can enlist your partner, best friend, or a family member to take on this journey with you. Tell each other about your long- and short-term financial goals, be honest about your current financial status, and help one another find actionable solutions to your biggest financial problems. In addition, you can make an arrangement to check on each other's progress in terms of saving, changing spending behaviors, and paying off loans and debts.

Your accountability partner is another person who will keep you within budget. Moreover, you can inspire each other to persist in pursuing financial freedom.

18. Put it in your savings.

If you somehow manage to spend less than the budget that you have set for yourself, congratulations! Now put that money into your savings account. You are not obliged to keep spending once you have paid all of your expected expenses. Do not spend on more MP2 and LP items just because you have money left in your budget.

19. Update your finance spreadsheet regularly.

When we discussed the four different budgeting techniques that you can implement in your life, I asked you to create a spreadsheet for your finances. Always update this spreadsheet, so you can see your financial status in real time. It is also practical to keep a list of everything you buy so you can input their costs into the spreadsheet at the end of each day. Doing so will prevent you from overspending and getting into unexpected debt.

20. Focus on your financial goals.

We cannot achieve all of our big financial goals in a short amount of time. Buying a house, sending your children to a good school, and saving for retirement do not happen overnight. Some of them will take us years to accomplish. But you must keep your focus and make financial decisions that will consistently take you one step closer to realizing your goals. Even if you are young and not planning on buying a house in the near future, start making plans on how you can reach this objective today.

WAYS TO SAVE MONEY WHILE ADOPTING A MINIMAL LIFESTYLE

Minimalism is a lifestyle that involves a conscious effort to live with less. You can say that it's like the barebones budgeting technique, i.e., you only surround yourself with material things that are necessary to your everyday life. You get rid of whatever does not serve your purpose, and you do not keep items for their sentimental value.

Minimalism, at its core, is a philosophy. The goal of adopting a minimalist lifestyle is to free yourself from the burdens that stem from materialism and consumerism. Instead of finding joy from possessions, you shift your mindset and focus on more important things such as family, relationships, community, and nature.

This philosophy has been present for hundreds of years. You can find examples of minimalism from Buddhist monks who renounced material possessions in the pursuit of higher spiritual awakening. They wear simple robes, sleep on mats on the floor, and eat food for nourishment, not gratification.

Today, this lifestyle has become a trend, especially among young professionals. More and more people are starting to live with less. You can see it in the growing popularity of tiny houses, which are usually between 100 and 400 square feet (Alterman, 2019). These small homes have the basics — a kitchen, a bathroom, a sleeping space, a living space — only much smaller. Every inch is optimized to serve a function.

Although minimalism has great advantages, let me tell you upfront that you do not need to adopt this lifestyle in order to achieve financial freedom. You do not have to get rid of your possessions or to move into a tiny house in order to become financially stable.

However, this philosophy does have elements that you can incorporate into your current lifestyle. These elements can transform your relationship with your possessions and make you less dependent on material things. As a result, you learn to make changes in your spending habits and to realign your financial decisions and goals.

Benefits of the Minimal Lifestyle

Why should you embrace the minimal lifestyle? I am going to let its benefits speak for themselves, so you can decide if you want to adopt minimalism or not.

Minimalism will eliminate your discontent while it teaches you to live with the essentials. As you slowly transition into it, you will realize that you have everything you need in order to live a full and well-functioning life. You will also come to realize that getting rid of the excess stuff is like achieving independence; you are not burdened by clutter anymore and you become free from constant want knowing that you already own what you need to survive.

Minimalism will reorient your priorities to the more important things in life. As you become less dependent on material possessions, you will realize that there is more to life than filling your home with things that society tells you you need. You will seek pleasure in building interpersonal relationships, in exploring the world around you, in finding new activities and hobbies you enjoy, etc. You will learn to live in the moment. You will want to spend your time doing more fulfilling things than staying at home with your stuff. Whatever you do not have at home, you will find them in the world outside. Moreover, you will develop a new sense of want—the want to learn and to grow as an individual.

Minimalism allows you to discover what your mission in life is. Because you are not tethered to material possessions, you will be free to pursue your passions. You will not be distracted by the accumulation of things. You will stop measuring your worth based on what you own. At the same time, you will have more resources to follow your heart and to start a new journey. Instead of allocating your time and money on acquiring new things, you can put them towards an interesting business venture or use them to fund a trip you have been dreaming of taking.

Do all of these sound good to you? They should! Although minimalism seems daunting in a world where consumerism is the norm, it actually has a lot of benefits that you can enjoy.

How to Adopt a Minimal Lifestyle

There is not a single set of rules to minimalism. However, the philosophy does lie on one basic principle: To live with less. You prioritize the essential stuff so you can strip away anything that does not bring value to your life. In terms of budgeting, minimalism is like paying off your HP and MP1 expenses first and then reducing your MP2 and LP expenses so that you can avoid debt and financial burdens.

Letting go of material things is a significant part of the process; although, it is not the most important aspect of minimalism. Do not forget the first part of the principle – to live. If cutting back gets in the way of your life, then you are defeating the purpose of minimalism.

Having said all that, here are five actionable steps to effectively transition into minimalism.

1. Analyze and prioritize

You begin the transition by looking at your life right now and analyzing what kind of relationship you have with your material possessions. During this step, you can use the same method of categorization that we used earlier to assess your expenses. Translate this method into how you look at your material possessions.

- High-priority (HP) items are things that you need and that are valuable to you.
- Mid-priority items are things that you need but

are not that valuable to you (MP1) or things that you value but are not necessary (MP2).
- Low-priority (LP) items are things that you do not need and are not valuable to you.

To give you an idea, the HP category will include clothes, shoes, and other personal items that you use regularly. It also covers kitchen and eating utensils, furniture pieces, gadgets, and the like. The MP1 category deals with the same subcategories as the HP category, but it includes items that you may not have used for a while and are collecting dust in your closet. Meanwhile, the MP2 category will include items that have sentimental value to you such as photographs and mementos. Lastly, the LP category will include any item that you can live without. Although this categorization will help you prioritize, it is still up to you to decide which items belong in each category.

During this step, you do not have to let go of your possessions yet. You just need to have a better understanding of what items are in your life right now. You might realize that you have a lot of MP1 items — clothes that you haven't worn for years or stuff that you didn't even realize was still in your closet. Or maybe you see that you like to keep MP2 things for their sentimental value, but you haven't found a way to keep them organized. The first step will reveal a lot about your relationship with your things like what you keep, what needs to be organized, and what you can survive without. This more profound comprehension will make the second step a lot easier.

2. Question yourself

Does this spark joy? Have I used this in the past year? The "spark joy" concept comes from Japanese author and organizing expert Marie Kondo. Her book, *Spark Joy: An Illustrated Master Class on the Art of Organizing and Tidying Up*, teaches its readers to organize by room and to only keep items that gives them a sudden burst of joy. This method allows you to still feel happy about the things you keep. As a result, letting go will not feel so heavy or difficult (Kondo, 2016).

The second question is a practical method that a lot of people I know use when decluttering their houses. I have personally asked myself this question when I would find it hard to depart from an item. If you haven't used something in the past year, there is really no good reason to keep it in your space anymore. It will just take up space in your house that you could use for more important things.

When you are on the fence about giving up an item, these questions will help you assess its value. No matter how difficult it may be, if you answered no to both of these questions, then it's time to let it go.

3. Be a mindful consumer

We have discussed mindfulness in earlier sections of this book. But this process is actually useful in adopting a minimalist lifestyle too.

Whenever you purchase something, you want it to add value to your life. So before you put it in your cart, ask yourself:

- How will this item serve you?
- Does it have an ulterior purpose?
- Do you currently own something similar to it?
- Do you expect to use it for a long time?
- Will you be getting a lot of use out of it?

Minimalism does not mean that you cannot buy new items or welcome new things in your life. But if you want to be a minimalist, you can't keep buying things out of impulse. You just need to be deliberate in every purchase.

4. Make more effective use of your time

In minimalism, you do not only prioritize efficiency in what you own but also in how you live your life. Remember that living is part of the philosophy. If you are chained to your material possessions, if they are hindering you from experiencing life, or if they take up a good chunk of your time, then you need to make some changes.

For example, our growing dependence on technology, gadgets, and social media has increasingly become a problem. On average, people around the world are on social media for at least an hour every day (Bridges, 2018). That's at least 365 hours of social media consumption in a year or 15 straight days of just scrolling through your different feeds.

With digital marketing getting more rampant in the age of the internet, it is normal to find advertisements on social networking sites. Brands have their own social media platforms where they market their products. They also partner and collaborate with influencers in selling their products and merchandise. If you are always on social media, you will more likely be tempted to purchase something you do not need.

So put down your screen. Take a walk outside. Hang out with friends and just live in the moment. You do not need to document every mundane activity on social media. The minimal lifestyle wants you to be in the present and to appreciate it before it fleets into the past.

5. Start small.

The last tip about minimalism that I will leave you with is to start small. If you are planning to adopt this lifestyle, it will most likely be a drastic change from how you are living right now. You will not be able to get rid of your material possessions in a day and that's okay. Take your time in transitioning until you are comfortable enough to fully embrace minimal living.

For the sake of transparency, I personally do not abide by

the minimal lifestyle. I still keep a box of junk from my college days purely for the nostalgia. However, I have managed to adopt some of its elements, using them to further my financial goals. I have seen how minimalism can change a person's attitude towards consumption and material possessions, and I can confidently say that it will be beneficial to at least use it as a guiding philosophy to how you live your life.

Saving Money with Minimalism

Now let's talk about how easy it is to save money when you adopt a minimal lifestyle. Minimalism can actually make saving so effortless. Before you know it, you are saving more than you ever had without even trying.

1. You spend deliberately.

With a minimal lifestyle, you become more deliberate in spending. Before any purchase, you become more thoughtful and conscientious. You will not purchase anything you do not need, so impulse buying becomes less and less frequent to the point that you are actually able to control your impulsive spending habits. You will also be able to apply this mindset in other expenses in your life, such as grocery shopping. You will find it easier to stick to your shopping list because you eliminate the craving to buy more stuff.

2. You save on mortgage or rent.

In adopting a minimal lifestyle, you will most likely reduce your belongings significantly. With fewer material possessions, you will need a smaller space to keep everything in. This is why minimalists love the tiny house movement. Aside from a smaller house that is easier to manage, less square footage means less mortgage or rent payments, which you can then put into your savings account or retirement fund. As a result, you are able to work on two major financial goals at once.

3. You save money on utilities and groceries.

Less stuff, smaller house, and fewer utilities — you will save money on electricity, water, and maintenance with minimal living. Your air-conditioning unit and heating system will need less power to make your space cool or warm. You will have fewer appliances also, which can further reduce your monthly electric bill. Plus, you will need less water and cleaning products to keep the house tidy. You will not have a lot of clothes to put in the laundry every week or dishes to wash every day. Imagine how much you can save on cleaning products alone when you go grocery shopping! You will also be more conscious of the food you buy at the grocery store because minimalism wants you to avoid waste. If you can't cook or consume a food item before it goes bad, don't put it in your cart.

4. You have more room in your budget to pay off debts.

As you embrace the minimal lifestyle, your budget will become more flexible with all the money you end up not spending. You can put the money you save from HP and MP1 expenses towards paying off debts.

5. You earn extra money by selling non-essential items.

Another great way to make your savings grow through minimalism is by selling items that you want to get rid of. You can have a garage sale or put up these items online. Alternatively, you can donate old clothes to charity so you can feel good about letting go of stuff.

These are just some of the ways that minimalism can help you build your savings and accomplish your financial goals. However, at the end of the day, you do not need to completely change your lifestyle. Like I said earlier, you can use this philosophy as a guide and implement some of its elements to make yourself less dependent on material things. By changing your fundamental way of thinking and looking at your possessions, you will realize that it is a lot easier to depart from consumerism than you originally thought.

THE GUILT-FREE WAY TO SPEND MONEY WHILE DOING WHAT YOU LOVE

Financial freedom is a long-term goal, but there is no reason as to why you can't do the things that you love right now. Although I am trying to help you form better spending habits, I also do not want you to deprive yourself of doing enjoyable things to the point that saving money becomes a burden instead of something that you actually want to do. Budgeting and saving money are positive things that will help you achieve financial freedom, so they should give you positive feelings.

At the same time, to have feelings of guilt with every purchase is almost as psychologically unhealthy as spending carelessly. After all, I do not want to turn you into an extremely frugal person. What I am trying to do with this book is to help you become a mindful consumer who always thinks about the implications of every financial decision to your overall financial goals. That is not equivalent to a restrained and inordinately simplistic life. I also want you to travel and to enjoy your youth while you are still young. You do not have to wait until you are retired to be able to experience the good things in life.

Therefore, in this section of the book, we will talk about removing the guilt in spending. How can you keep doing what you love without feeling guilty every time you spend money? I will also introduce a new way to look at your purchasing behavior. But before we dive into the reformation process, let's first discuss where these feelings of guilt may come from.

The Guilt of Spending

Based on personal experience, I would usually feel guilt and other negative emotions when I spend money on MP2 and LP items that I did not anticipate in my budget. Yes, I am also guilty of impulse buying. I used to be an impulsive buyer before I started being mindful of where I allocate my resources. Today, there are still times when I purchase an item that was not listed on my budget. But because of my healthier habits around money, I always have the funds to buy something from the store in the rare occasions that I get the itch to. As a result, I do not feel guilty about how I spend my money anymore.

But for someone like you who is just starting to form new and more sustainable financial habits, I would understand if you still cave into impulses and feel guilty about them after the fact. This happens to everybody! However, have you ever wondered why impulse buying is such a common thing?

Like most impulsive behaviors, buying without careful thought is actually a result of positive emotions, such as pleasure and excitement, which you initially associate with a thing that you see at the store. Most people would believe that it is the other way around, that impulse buying results to positive feelings. However, these good feelings are actually pre-consumption emotions. Meanwhile, regret, guilt, and other negative feelings associated with impulse buying are usually post-consumption emotions. According to Miao (2016), these responses are "rooted in basic human thought processes that either encourage or discourage impulsive behavior." In other words, that feeling of guilt may be your mind reminding you that you did something you shouldn't have done. At the same time, the exhilaration you associate with impulse buying makes it more challenging to break this bad habit.

Bauer, Wilkie, Kim, and Bodenhausen (2012) also reached the same conclusions about consumerism. Their experiments proved that a materialistic mindset can have negative consequences to a person's overall well-being. In fact, it can also be detrimental to one's social engagement; isolation, competitiveness, and mistrust against other people arise from consumerist behavior because material possessions automatically boost one's perception of self. It's "the more I have, the better off I am" way of thinking. The researchers also discovered that aside from positive pre-consumption feelings, widespread cues that exist in everyday life, such as advertising, heavily influence a person's spending behavior.

Lastly, Alonso, Rodriguez, and Rojo (2015) examined consumerist behavior in relation to the economic crisis in Spain. The results of their study support the findings of Bauer et al. (2012) in terms of the negative effects of consumerism to one's social behavior. When they asked their subjects about irrational spending behaviors, they were quick to point to others' excessive consumption. Shifting blame is particularly notable in the upper class; they believed that consumerism led to Spain's economic crisis, although they refused to take accountability for their own behaviors. What I gather from this study is that a materialistic mindset has negative consequences not only to self-perception but also to an individual's perception of the people around them.

With these feelings of guilt, people develop even worse spending behaviors because they associate money with negative emotions. They tend to become more impulsive because they chase the short high that comes from anticipation and excitement over a new purchase. Like an addiction, you crave for the positive pre-consumption emotions that result from impulse buys. It's a cycle of behavior that can easily put you into unmanageable debt.

This is why I want you to stop feeling guilty when you spend money. Any and all unhealthy behaviors involving money will prevent you from achieving financial freedom in the long run. As you form better financial habits and slowly find stability, you should be able to spend money consciously and without guilt.

Freedom from Guilt

So how can you spend money without guilt? There are

certain steps you can follow, which I will teach you later on. For now, there is an exercise that I want you to do.

On a piece of paper, answer this question: Why do I buy impulsively? List all the possible reasons you can think of — depression, stress, excessive need, excessive desire, etc. Whatever your reasons may be, write them down and be as detailed as you can. It will help if you look at the items that you have bought without deliberation and think back to the specific situation that led you to purchase it.

The purpose of this exercise is for you to have a clear vision of why you have an impulsive spending habit. You may see patterns of behavior on the list that you have written. For example, you may find that you are likely to purchase things impulsively if you have had a hard week at work. You may be using money (or the things that you buy with money) as a reward for your efforts even though there is a possibility of going over budget and, in some cases, being in debt.

Read through your list and find repetitive causes that lead you to spend beyond your budget. The first step you can take in order to eliminate money-related guilt is to find other ways to deal with these issues.

Going back to the example earlier, you can reward yourself after a long and difficult work week by giving yourself a day to relax. Play some soothing music, put on a face mask, and have a nice warm bath. You can also spend a day outdoors, chilling at the park or walking in nature, if it eases the itch to shop. It is up to you to decide what activities can curve your impulsive buying behaviors. Doing pleasurable activities can take your mind off whatever it is that you don't need, but want, to buy.

Aside from finding other outlets for your impulses, here are other actionable steps that you can take to free yourself from guilt.

1. If you really want it, go buy it.

You may have had your eyes on an expensive thing for a while now. Maybe it's a new couch or a luxury clothing item. The price tag has stopped you from making the purchase, but it is still consistently on your mind. If this is the case, it is not an impulse buy and you should be able to find a way to fit it in your budget. How? Well, you can reassess your future expenses and look for certain items that you can cut for a while so you can save enough money for this one big purchase that you really want to make. Remember that the root cause of spending-related guilt is impulsive behavior. Therefore, consciously adjusting your budget to buy this item should not bring you negative post-consumption emotions.

2. Make room for the fun stuff.

Unless you are in a grave crisis, like sudden unemployment or a medical emergency, there is no reason for you to deprive yourself of the fun stuff. Make room in your budget for going out to a bar with your friends, seeing a concert, or visiting a museum. Aside from being fun, these activities will bring you other positive feelings which can help you cope with negative circumstances that often lead you to impulse buy.

3. Learn to say no.

Learn to say no to things that bring you short-term happiness. If you are going to spend your money, put it towards something that will bring you joy for a much longer time. For example, material things go in and out of style. But experiences, like traveling to a new place, will give you stories to tell and memories that you get to bring with you for the rest of your life.

4. Evaluate your motivations.

You learned earlier that impulses are triggered by circumstances in your life that are often negative. But spending-related guilt doesn't just come from impulse buying. Even when the purchase is deliberate, you may feel guilty about it afterwards. Most of the time, the reason for this is the underlying motivation of the purchase, especially when you use shopping as a form of therapy.

You need to realize that "retail therapy" is often counterintuitive. Instead of making you feel better, the dent in your budget brings forth negative emotions that put you in a worse emotional state.

So think about it this way, you cannot solve a problem with another problem. If you are using shopping as a coping mechanism to an issue that you currently have, you will not be able to feel good about your financial habits. "Money can't buy happiness" is a statement that is as real as the issues that you are trying to pacify with the items in your cart.

Additionally, if you buy things to get praise and attention from other people, you will develop an unsustainable shopping habit. These positive affirmations from other people can make you think that shopping all the time is a good thing. Plus, you may become dependent on compliments, which is bad for your mental health.

5. Sleep on it.

When I browse the internet, I always see advertisements for things that I do not need. Often, I think of them as a nuisance. But there are also times when I see something that attracts me like a moth to an open flame. This rare happenstance triggers the impulsive consumerist in me. He wakes up from a deep slumber with his eyes wide open and shouts, "Go get it!"

In this situation, I always try to sleep on it. I do not make any decisions until I've rested for the night. The next day, I will have a fresher mind and, most of the time, the impulse to buy is gone. This passing urge tells me a lot about why I had it in the first place. It reveals to me that what attracted me to the product is not the product itself but how it was advertised.

I have come to realize that this is true for a lot of people.

We've all purchased an item because it looked good on the advertisement. Remember, this is exactly what advertisements do. They present a product in the best light to fool consumers into thinking that we need it in our lives. So the next time you see something on an ad that you want to buy, go to bed and sleep on it first.

TIPS FROM THE EXPERTS: WHAT MILLIONAIRES KNOW ABOUT BUDGETING THAT YOU DON'T

Here's the secret to become a millionaire: Apply everything you have learned so far in this book. That's it. No tricks. I've said it in the very beginning – the key to financial freedom is to lay a stable foundation involving money management. Once you have mastered it, the rest will fall into place eventually. You will see your finances grow in no time and accomplish your long-term financial goals as you have planned.

Just to give you a solid blueprint on how to manage your finances like a millionaire, here are 12 steps that you can take towards financial freedom.

1. Prioritize your needs.

In an earlier section of this book, I have taught you a foolproof scheme to categorizing your expenses. Your HP and MP1 expenses are the necessities; these are things that you can't live without. Meanwhile, your MP2 and LP expenses are the non-essentials; in times of financial emergency, these are things that you can cut from your budget in order to make room for more important stuff.

In building your foundation, you need to learn to differentiate between your needs and wants. Even if an item falls under your HP or MP1 expenses, it can still be influenced by unnecessary desires. Food, for example, is a high-priority expense. However, if you always eat at overpriced restaurants instead of cooking at home or finding cheaper alternatives, you will continue making bad financial decisions that can break your budget and put you in a cycle of instability.

At the same time, you should not deprive yourself of your needs just to make room for your wants. Starving yourself to buy an expensive designer item doesn't sound like a good financial decision, does it? If you are sacrificing your overall well-being in pursuit of lavish things, you are making the wrong decisions. With every choice you have to make, prioritize your needs.

2. Stick to your budget.

This step sounds a lot easier than it actually is, especially for beginners. Budgeting is a habit that you need to form, and not all habits are easily established. When you start your journey towards financial freedom, this will be one of the most challenging things you need to go through, but it can be done. And when it is done, you will realize that every sacrifice is worth it.

A simple trick to stick to your budget: Do not be so rigid about it. If you use a time-based budgeting technique, let's say on a monthly basis, you do not have to implement the same budget structure from month to month. Maybe you are not spending as much on food as you thought, so allocate those unused funds somewhere else. Maybe you could be saving more. Maybe you could be earning more. The key is to keep analyzing your spreadsheets in order to find ways to improve your current budget structure.

3. Spend deliberately.

I have mentioned this tip several times before, but it is one of the most effective ways to take control of your finances. Every purchase decision must be thought out, no matter how small it is, because none of your expenses are insignificant. They are all influenced by your spending behavior, and so you need to practice mindfulness for all of them if you want to establish better spending habits.

Here are a few things you can do to be more deliberate in

spending:

- Create a shopping list and only buy items that are on it.
- Eliminate redundant expenses.
- Find cheaper alternatives.
- Do not purchase something you can borrow.
- Consider the quality of the product as well as the quantity of use that you will get out of it.
- Do not spend more than what you earn.

4. Track your expenses.

In connection to the previous step, you should also track your expenses to have a better understanding of your spending habits. I have mentioned earlier how keeping receipts and transaction records can help you monitor where your money is going.

What you can also do is to download budgeting apps that track your expenses in real time. In some apps, you have the option to integrate your bank account so you can get notifications whenever you pay a bill or make a purchase.

We will discuss some of my favorite budgeting apps in more detail in Chapter 2 of this book.

5. Live below your means.

Even though some millionaires drive fancy cars and live in big mansions, they still know what it means to live below their means. They do not spend their whole monthly income. In most cases, they save or invest more than what they spend. The reason they can own fancy cars and big mansions is simply because they can; these luxuries do not detract from their overall financial goals.

Those of us who do not belong in the 1% can learn from these millionaires. Live below your means and save the luxuries for when you make your first million. Maybe not even then. Maybe you will learn how to enjoy the simpler things in life while you watch your savings grow. Who cares if you are driving an old car? If it's still capable of taking you to places without breaking down, then it's good enough. You do not need a Tesla Model Y or a Lamborghini Huracan. Treat your current possessions like they are your old friends and you will find it harder to replace them.

To know what it's like to live below your means, remember what you learned from when we talked about minimalism. You will definitely benefit from adopting this philosophy and using some of its elements in your current lifestyle.

6. Avoid debt.

If you learn how to spend deliberately and to live below your means, you will find it easier to avoid debt. What you probably realize by now is that establishing better spending habits will create a ripple effect throughout your overall financial status. When you overcome your impulsive buying behavior and learn how to control your expenses, you will have more funds to pay off existing debts and to avoid future debts at the same time.

7. Have a contingency plan.

Emergencies are inevitable. Worse, they are unpredictable. To make sure you do not go into debt when a personal or a medical crisis happens, have a contingency plan.

My advice is for you to set up a savings account that you will slowly but steadily fill with at least six months' worth of expenses. In the case of sudden unemployment or inability to work, you have enough funds to get you going until you find a stable source of income once again.

A contingency plan prevents you from dipping into your long-term savings for when something unexpected happens. It will help protect your overall financial goals even in the face of a crisis.

8. Automate bills and investments.

In Chapter 2 of this book, I will give you more details about how financial automation can change your life as well as how you can effectively implement it. For now, here is a quick overview of why you should automate.

First of all, automating bill payments and investment contributions will unload the burden of manually managing your finances. It ensures that you are paying bills on time, which helps you to avoid late payment fees and surcharges as well as to improve your credit score. It also aids in creating good money habits in terms of saving; you can automatically transfer an amount to your savings account or retirement fund when you receive your monthly paycheck. Plus, brokerage firms are now offering automated investment payment options that automatically adjust your asset allocation based on your portfolio.

9. Have multiple sources of income.

Whether you are a freelancer or a 9-to-5 employee, there are some ways that you can earn a little extra on the side. One of the smartest financial decisions you can make is to invest. We will discuss investing for beginners in Chapter 2.

Aside from investing, you can also work side gigs that will allow you to earn more money. Here are a couple of ideas:

- Start a small business. For example, if you are good at baking, you can turn this skill into a profitable side hustle. You can accept orders for cupcakes, cookies, or muffins when you have time off work. You can also charge more if customers have special requests. By turning something you love into a business, you get to enjoy what you do instead of feeling burdened by the additional responsibility. And who knows? Maybe this little venture can become a full-time business in the future.
- Open an online store for pre-loved items. You can

turn your pre-loved items into additional income by selling them online. This enables you to let go of material possessions that are not valuable to you anymore in a more productive and profitable way. Plus, managing an online store is easy, at least when compared to managing a physical shop. You won't have to pay for rent and the business hours are more flexible. So even if you have a regular job, you can still run your business through your smartphone or laptop.
- Accept commission work. For those who have artistic talents, use them to earn extra income. You can accept commissions from local businesses who want new logo designs or need posters and signages made. To start making money, set up an online portfolio where potential customers can see how talented you are. Do not forget to put your contact information so they know how to reach you. Like an online store, you can manage this business venture through the internet.

10. Do not be afraid to ask for help.

When you are having a particularly challenging time in managing your finances, do not be afraid to ask for advice from the experts. They do not have to be a professional financial adviser like me. Maybe you have a friend who is well versed in investments or has a good track in saving money. Pick their brain and maybe you can find the solution to whatever financial dilemma you are currently dealing with. It is not shameful to admit that you have a problem. Asking for help is an important step in getting better at anything in life.

11. Always educate yourself.

You are reading this book right now, which means the desire to learn is already there. Props to you for that! This is already a major step towards financial stability. However, there is always something new to learn. After you finish this book, my hope is that you continue to educate yourself about the different ways that you can better manage your finances.

12. Keep your eyes on the goal.

I have said this before but I will say it again: Keep your eyes on your long-term financial goals. Do not get distracted by short-term thrills that do not add value to your life or that do not help you move towards financial freedom, especially if you are at a point in your life where you are still trying to find stability. Lavish things and other luxuries can wait until you are on solid ground financially.

And with that, we are done discussing the basics of personal financial management. Try to remember everything you have learned thus far so that you can apply these techniques in real life and build a strong foundation that will take you closer to financial freedom.

BUILD WEALTH AND RUN A SUCCESSFUL BUSINESS WITHOUT LEAVING YOUR FAMILY LIFE ASIDE

It's time to build the house. In this chapter, we will discuss the different ways that you can build your wealth without sacrificing the most important thing in your life — your family.

I have seen this struggle way too often. Children feel neglected by parents who are working regular jobs and managing small businesses on the side. Finding a balance between business and family seem very challenging for a lot of people. Even those without children are struggling to keep healthy personal and social lives because of their desire to make more.

There's nothing wrong about wanting to increase your income. But financial freedom is all about minimizing, if not eliminating, your financial burdens. If you are earning more money by putting your relationships at risk, then you are not living by the philosophy that I have been trying to teach you since the beginning.

So how do you find balance? How can you keep earning additional income without jeopardizing your personal, social, and family lives? Let me teach you in this chapter.

AUTOMATE YOUR FINANCES AND SAVE MONEY WHILE BUILDING WEALTH AND ABUNDANCE

With the abundance of financial technology and applications today, automating your finances has become a lot easier. You can spend less time manually managing your finances or worrying about where your money is going if you use the right tools. In this section of the book, we will talk about financial automation, its benefits, and how you can properly use it to manage your finances.

Why should you automate your finances?

How many hours in a week, a month, or a year do you spend balancing books, updating spreadsheets, paying bills and taxes, and managing all of your financial activities? It may not seem like a lot if you look at the big picture, or maybe you are spending way too much time on these tasks than you'd like. Either way, I think you can make better use of your time.

The main benefit of automating your finances is that you get to spend less time on money management. The time you save from these tasks can then be reallocated to operating your business or, better yet, to spending more quality time with your family. You can also perform day-to-day tasks without getting interrupted by paying bills or worrying about late payments. If you use the right tools, they will pay all of your bills for you right on schedule.

Another amazing benefit of financial automation is that you do not forget to pay yourself first. You have the option to transfer money into your savings account as soon as your paycheck comes in. You can also automatically pay retirement fund contributions and investment payments through a financial app.

Efficiency is the key benefit of financial automation. Aside from a more productive use of your time, the right tools will integrate your data. You can easily access your data through these apps and get a clear picture of your cash flow, expenditure breakdown, and savings status. Most apps will also send you real time notifications whenever payments are made. In addition, you can control your budget through these apps and see how much money you are allowed to spend before you go over-budget. With these features, you are able to make wiser financial decisions that contribute to your short- and long-term stability.

Moreover, financial automation ensures that you are paying credit card bills and other debts consistently and on time. This prevents you from getting into more debt by paying additional fees, shouldering interest, and facing other surcharges for late payments. As time passes by, you will realize how effective financial automation is in reducing debts.

The bottom line: Financial automation helps you to make more efficient use of your time and to prioritize your savings, expenses, and debts before you spend money on non-essential items.

How can you automate your finances?

Now that you know how financial automation can benefit your life, let me show you how to properly put it in action. I am giving you four simple steps to guide you through the process.

1. Set up accounts.

The first thing you need to do is to set up your accounts, beginning with a checking account if you do not already have one. This is the control center of your finances; money will come in and go out of this account after you have completed setting up your entire financial automation plan.

The second account you need to set up is your savings account. You can set up different accounts for long-term savings and contingency savings, which we discussed in an earlier section of the book. The latter is what you will use to pay your bills and other expenses in the case of sudden unemployment or medical crisis. If you have any other short-term savings goal (like saving up for a home, a car, or a vacation), you can make a separate account for this too. Alternatively, use a financial app to track these different savings goals so you can keep them all in one bank account.

Speaking of which, you should also download financial tools that will help you keep track of your cash flow and savings. Some of my personal favorites include the following:

- Simple is more than just an online bank. It is also an app that has features aimed to help you stay within budget. For instance, it's Safe-to-Spend feature allows you to input an amount that you can flexibly spend for a given time period. With this feature, you do not have to compute or make adjustments in your budget whenever you want to purchase something. You also do not have to worry that you are going over budget because the app updates you on how much money is still safe to spend. Therefore, it can really help you in eliminating the guilt in spending, which we discussed in the first chapter. When you make a Simple account, you get a debit card along with it. However, Simple is currently only available in the United States. It does not charge you a monthly fee.
- Chime is also an online bank that comes with a debit card, a spending account, and a savings account. With Chime, you can have a clear picture of your spending activities in real time. When you open the app, you will see your spending balance and savings balance. You can also see a detailed list of every transaction you make using your Chime debit card. In fact, you will get a notification through the app whenever you make a purchase.

This helps you keep track of bill and utility payments that you have automated through the app. Like Simple, Chime is currently only available in the United States and does not charge a monthly fee.

- You Need a Budget is a comprehensive budgeting app that forces you to consider every dollar that comes in and goes out of your account. Some would say that it's the perfect budgeting app for people with Type-A personalities because of how detail-oriented it is. It breaks down your expenses into categories and allows you to transfer money from income sources into bank accounts. Personally, the only negative traits that I see about You Need a Budget is that it has a monthly fee and that it takes a while to fully understand the interface of the app. But once you get it, it will be easy to track inflow, outflow, and savings. You can also integrate your existing bank accounts into the app if you live in the United States and Canada.

2. Pay yourself first.

After you have set up your checking and savings accounts and financial management tools, the next thing you need to do is to come up with a savings scheme that you can then input into the apps. My advice is for you to automate your retirement fund contributions and to make automatic transfers to your savings account. If you have investment payments, automate them during this step too. A lot of financial apps will let you set recurring payments on a weekly, bimonthly, monthly, or yearly basis.

The reason why I want you to pay yourself first is simple. Your savings contribute to your long-term financial goals. Therefore, by setting aside this portion of your income, you are not tempted to postpone them to make room for more urgent needs. Even though you may not be close to retirement age, saving for the future is still an important aspect of achieving financial freedom.

3. Pay expenses.

Once you have paid yourself, pay your expenses next. Like your savings and retirement fund, you can also automate bills and other payments through financial apps.

My advice for this step is to group your expenses based on their due dates. Pay all bills that have close deadlines on the earliest due date so you only receive one payment notification from the app. Turn on the "recurring payment" feature, if available, so you won't have to manually schedule each payment every time the due date is close.

Unfortunately, for bills that change amounts from month-to-month like your phone and electricity bills, you will have to adjust their value on the app manually. Or you can overestimate their value if you want to completely automate them. The charging company will deduct any advanced payments from the next bill.

4. Increase savings over time.

Most people's debts grow into unmanageable proportions because of late credit card payments. Instead of being able to save a fixed percentage of their income, they put that money towards credit card fees and surcharges. As I mentioned earlier, financial automation can actually help you avoid this problem. You are able to avoid additional costs because your payments are consistent and always on time. As these expenses decrease over time, you will notice that you have more room in your budget. But wait! Do not fill the void in your budget where your credit card bills and debts used to be with new expenses! Instead, you can adjust your monthly savings and put more money into this account. The more you save, the closer you get to financial freedom.

INVESTING FOR ABSOLUTE BEGINNERS: LEARN THE BASICS

In every economy, there is inflation. The inflation rate measures the rate by which the prices of goods and services increase over time. This usually goes up and down depending on how strong the economy is, but the common trend for inflation in the long run is upwards. Through time, the cost of living becomes more and more expensive. The rent for a one-bedroom apartment in your city cost significantly less 50years ago than it does today. The same goes for the prices of groceries, gas, and other basic needs. So even if you stick to a barebones budget and only buy the essentials in the coming years, your cost of living will still be higher than it is at the moment. In other words, if you generate the same salary in the foreseeable future, you will not be able to build your wealth or achieve financial freedom due to inflation.

Let's say you have $10,000 in your account. The purchasing power of that amount will not be the same in 10 years because of inflation. If you do not do something to make those $10,000 grow, then you will actually lose money because this amount will not be as valuable as it is today.

The best thing about investing your money is that it grows over time. Let's say the return on investment is 10% compounded annually. In a year, that will make your $10,000 grow to $11,000. In 10 years, you will have $110,000! That's like earning $100,000 without lifting a finger! (Note: This is just an example. Investment rates are not always 10% compounded annually, and there are other factors that affect your investments. But you see the point, right? Investing your money effectively builds your wealth.)

If you start investing early, you will reap the rewards earlier as well. Going back to the example earlier, say the maturity period of your investment is 10 years. If you start investing at 25 years old, you will receive $110,000 by the time you are 35 years old! You can then use this amount to put a down payment on a house or to start your own business.

You can also look at it this way: If you decide to withdraw your funds from the investment only when you retire at 60 years old, then that money will continue to grow. Ceteris paribus, your initial $10,000 investment will become $385,000 in 35 years! Doesn't that sound like a sweet retirement fund?

Now let's circle back for a second on how investing early can benefit you and apply that ideology to a retirement fund. If you start investing at 25 years old, you will receive a heftier amount at retirement than, say, if you start investing at 40 years old. Using the same variables, your initial investment of $10,000 will only become $220,000 in 20 years. That's a $165,000 difference. To earn $385,000, you will have to wait until you are 75 years old.

The bottom line is that you should invest, and if possible, you should invest as early as you can. Time is your friend when it comes to investing. The sooner you put in money, the sooner you reap the reward or the bigger the reward is.

This is just a general idea of how investing can help you build wealth. In the next section of the book, I will teach you about the different types of investments that you can put your money in.

Types of Investments

There are three primary types of investments: stocks, bonds, and commodities. We will go through each of them to see how they can help you achieve your financial goals.

Stocks

Stocks are what you "buy" from the stock market, which usually refer to common stock or business equity. In simplest terms, you buy a portion of a business when you buy a stock, which technically makes you one of the owners of the business. However, your ownership of the business is often limited to sharing the profits or losses that it generates through its different income-generating venues. This is called a preferred stock. Consider yourself a silent partner. You do not have voting power when you buy this type of stock.

In some cases, when you buy common shares from a company, you will get voting rights and act as a shareholder. One share of common stock usually gives you one voting power. You can invest in this type of stock as well but, for the sake of our discussion, we will refer to preferred stocks when we talk about stocks.

Anyone can buy a stock from a private business once it decides to sell through an Initial Public Offering (IPO). To invest in a stock, you will most likely hire a brokerage firm to manage your portfolio. A brokerage firm is a financial institution that acts as a middleman between you (the buyer) and the business (the seller). It earns through commissions, so you will have to pay a fee for any transaction the firm makes on your behalf. Although the brokerage firm manages your portfolio, you still get to make the major decisions and control your investments, like where you want to put your money or if you want to buy or sell.

Here's a pro tip for you: Stock picking (or choosing individual companies to buy stocks from) is not a good idea for a lot of people, even if the companies you like to invest in are part of the Fortune 500. Investing in individual companies like this expose you to major risks. How? Well, let's take a look at the largest market cap losses in big cap stocks in history (Imbert & Francolla, 2018):

- JP Morgan Chase lost $2,488,418,000 in 2008.
- Citigroup Inc. lost $2,594,123,000 in 2002.
- Wells Fargo lost $2,890,581,000 in 2018.
- Amazon lost $3,647,745,000 in 2018.

- Bank of America lost $3,848,679,000 in 2008.
- Alphabet lost $4,107,484,000 in 2018.
- General Electric lost $4,691,475,000 in 2008.
- Exxon Mobil lost $5,251,138,000 in 2008.
- Apple lost $5,963,368,000 in 2013.
- Microsoft lost $8,003,460,000 in 2000.
- Intel lost $9,073,696,000 in 2000.
- Finally, the biggest market cap loss in big cap stocks belong to Facebook which lost a whopping $11,941,931,000 in 2018 following a 19% decline in its stock price.

To avoid taking part in these losses, you need to diversify when investing in stocks. You can also choose mutual and index funds instead of picking stocks individually. We will discuss these in more detail later on.

Bonds

In a nutshell, bonds are low-risk, fixed-income investments. When you invest in a bond, you are "lending" money to the borrower (which will depend on what type of bond you choose). The money you invest, called the principal, will be returned to you at the maturity date. While waiting for the investment to mature, you will receive interest payments from the borrower.

There are different types of bonds based on who issues them. Generally, you can invest in treasury bonds, municipal bonds, and corporate bonds. The first type is issued by the national government and offers the lowest risk but also the least interest. There are further subcategories of treasury bonds, but the most common takes 30 years to mature.

The second type is issued by local governments. It yields more interest than the treasury bonds, but it has slightly higher risks. There are short-term municipal bonds, which mature between one to three years, and long-term municipal bonds, which take at least a decade to mature. The interest you earn from municipal bonds are usually exempt from federal taxes, which is one of its advantages. In some cases, you can also deduct interest income from municipal bonds from your local taxes if you get the bond from your local government.

Lastly, corporate bonds yield the highest interest among the three types of bonds. However, they also come with the most risk because the issuer of the bond can't simply raise taxes to be able to pay the money it borrowed. Like municipal bonds, there are short-term and long-term corporate bonds.

Another interesting thing about bonds is that you can sell them before they mature. You can earn money by selling the bond at higher than the principal. However, depending on the type of bond that you invested in, there's also a possibility that you will lose money if you sell it before maturity.

Commodities

I normally do not advise beginners to start their investments with commodities. But just to give you an idea of what investing in commodities entail, here is a quick overview.

There are two ways in which you can invest in commodities. One, you can purchase physical raw commodities for trading, or two, you can invest in commodity stocks which are tracked based on a specific commodity index. Either way, you are dealing with volatile investments because they both involve the basic economic principle of supply and demand, which directly affect the prices of commodities. Other factors also come into play, like import and government regulations, political instability, etc.

At the same time, commodity investments also have benefits. For one, they are positively affected by higher inflation rates, which often cause stocks and bonds to deflate. Because higher inflation drives up commodity prices, this can be a good thing for your investment.

Nonetheless, I still would not recommend for you to

invest in commodities if you are just starting out. Compared to stocks and bonds, there are more factors to consider and more data to analyze. You can still choose to consult with a brokerage firm to see whether investing in commodities is a good idea. At the end of the day, with any type of investment, you just need to make informed decisions to avoid losing money and to maximize returns.

Diversify

You may have heard the phrase "don't put your eggs in one basket" before. But do you understand what it means?

Quite literally, if one basket happens to topple over and the eggs in it crack, you still have eggs safe in other baskets.

In the context of investment, what this means is that you have to divide your resources into different investment types so that you can minimize the risks involved. As a general rule, you want to diversify your investment by finding the right balance between stocks and bonds. This allows you to have a financial cushion in case some of your stocks perform badly. This also allows you to increase your gains because different stocks have different interest yields that vary over time.

Index Funds versus Mutual Funds

Now, let's talk about index funds and mutual funds. What are their differences? Which one is better? These are just some of the questions that we will be answering right now. To start, let's define what these two types of funds are.

Mutual Funds

Mutual funds are called as they are because they are a mutual portfolio shared by several investors. The investors pool their money and then a fund manager puts that collective investment towards a selection of stocks and bonds. If you buy a share of mutual funds, you are buying a portion of the value of the portfolio, not just a stock from a company or a bond from the government.

What this means is that you start your investment with an

already diversified portfolio. (Remember what I said about diversification?) This is one of the advantages of investing in a mutual fund instead of picking individual stocks or bonds.

Moreover, pooling resources from several investors allow each person to invest at a significantly lower entry point. While most principals are worth thousands of dollars for just one company, you will be able to start investing on a portfolio at a fraction of the cost.

Another advantage of mutual funds is that you do not have to personally manage it. Like I said earlier, there is a fund manager who handles the portfolio. Fund managers are experts in the stock market. They make decisions for the benefit of the whole pool so that everyone's interest income can be maximized.

Index Funds

As the name suggests, the value of an index fund mimics the index it is tracking. It can actually refer to mutual funds or exchange-traded funds whose goal is to match the returns of its respective index. When you invest in an index fund, you are also investing in a diversified portfolio.

There are a lot of market indexes that dictate the value of index funds. Some measure the stock exchange performance of small-cap companies, like the Russell 2000, while others measure the stock exchange performance of large-cap companies, like the S&P 500. The most important thing to remember is that one index fund is specific to one market index. Therefore, if your index fund tracks the S&P 500, it will not change its value based on other indexes.

Investing in index funds has several advantages. One, it usually has lower fees than a mutual fund because the fund manager does not need to perform as much research and analysis given the fact that an index fund simply replicates its benchmark index. In addition, they do not need to make as many trades as a mutual fund manager would, which further brings down the operations cost.

Index funds are also generally passive. Neither you nor the fund manager need to make constant adjustments based on how one or a few of the stocks are performing.

Which is better?

Index and mutual funds have two main differences — management and expense ratio.

As I mentioned earlier, an index fund requires passive management. The fund manager does not have to keep adjusting or trading stocks in order to achieve the fund's objective. On the other hand, a mutual fund requires constant attention and analysis.

You might be wondering, "Why should I care about the management of these funds? Isn't that what a fund manager is for?"

Well, the more involved the fund manager is, the higher the related costs, fees, and commissions. These factors drive up the expense ratio of mutual funds. Even though a mutual fund may perform better in terms of returns than an index fund, the brokerage firm will have to deduct these expenses before you receive income from the investment.

For beginners, I would suggest that you invest in index funds first. This is a great starting point, especially if you are still trying to learn about investments. As you get a better understanding of how it all works, you should be able to slowly transition into more active types of investments.

DANGEROUS MONEY MYTHS WE NEED TO BUST RIGHT AWAY

Part of changing your overall attitude towards money is to stop believing dangerous money myths that are detrimental in your journey towards financial freedom. Let's go through 10 of the most common false beliefs about money and debunk each of them.

1. Investing is for rich people

You do not need to have a six-figure annual income to be able to start investing. You don't have to wait until you reach a certain level of income either. In fact, it is advisable to start investing as young as you can. As you have learned in the previous section, investing is a great way to build your wealth. The sooner you start investing, the sooner you can reap the rewards.

2. Savings = Income - Expenses

You learned in the first chapter of this book that savings should be a priority every single time you receive your paycheck. Before you pay any of your bills or budget for the month, you should take a fixed percentage of your salary and put that towards your savings account. In other words, pay yourself first.

If your budget is a little tight this month, you should not deduct from your savings. You will find more room in your budget by removing certain MP2 and LP expenses. You should avoid spending money on these non-essentials until you have a more solid footing on your finances again.

3. Savings Account = Contingency Fund

You should have separate accounts for your long- and short-term savings plans, so you won't have to withdraw from your long-term savings in the case of an emergency. You need to prepare a standalone contingency fund that you can use if ever you lose your source of income or need additional money to pay for medical costs and other similar emergencies. As I mentioned earlier, the general rule in preparing a contingency fund is to set up an account containing six months' worth of essential expenses. If you need to reduce MP2 and LP expenses for a while so you can save enough for this, you should. You can reintroduce these non-essential expenses in your budget as soon as you have completed your contingency fund.

4. Credit Card = Contingency Fund

In the same context, you should not use your credit card

as an emergency fall back. It is counterintuitive to use a credit card when you do not have a stable source of income for two reasons. One, you are borrowing money beyond your ability to pay. Two, what you owe will multiply given its interest rate, which will make it even more difficult to pay given your situation. In the case of an emergency, it is actually advisable to avoid credit card transactions. This is why you need to save up for a contingency fund so you have something to fall back on.

5. Invest in real estate

Yes, almost everyone wants to invest in real estate as part of their long-term financial goals. Even if you decide to sell the property in the future, you can earn on top of what you paid for by making improvements to the house. However, there is also the possibility that the property's value will decrease over time. A real estate investment is also a non-liquid asset. In other words, you cannot just turn it into cash if you are in sudden need of funds.

Like every other financial decision, you need to weigh the pros and cons of investing in real estate. It is a huge commitment to buy a property. Make sure that you thought it through and considered all the factors before making an offer.

6. Going for the cheaper alternative

I told you earlier to look for cheaper alternatives whenever you can. However, cheaper isn't always better. You need to look not only at the price tag of a product but also at its quality. Will you be able to use it for a long time? In terms of functionality and longevity, does it compare to the brand name product that you want to buy? Or is its affordable price tag a reflection of its poor quality?

Even if you keep buying cheaper products, if you have to replace them every couple of months or so, then you are not making a good financial decision. It is good to cut costs when shopping but do not choose the more affordable option for the sake of saving money immediately.

7. Waiting to Save for retirement

You should save for retirement as soon as you get hired on your first job as a fresh graduate. Let me explain why.

Let's say that you want to retire by the time you are 60. By then, you predict that you already have a house and a car and that your kids have graduated from college. (You won't have to start a family until you are at least in your mid-30s for this scenario to be real.) If you are currently 25 years old, you will have 35 years to save for retirement.

Now let's say that you plan on saving $6,000 a year for your retirement fund. In 35 years, you will have $210,000 flat. On the other hand, someone your age who only starts saving 10 years later will have $150,000 flat.

If you start to save for retirement at an earlier age, you will also have more time to make your retirement fund grow. You will have 10 years' worth of interest over the other person in this example. Given an arbitrary 5% compounded interest, this is what your retirement fund will look like in 35 years: $602,114.03. Meanwhile, the other person will have $320,998.85 by 60 years old, which is almost half of what you have!

8. Use your credit card for the rewards

You will learn later on about the different ways you can use your credit card to your advantage. For now, let me give you a quick advice: Do not use your credit cards to "chase rewards. Yes, you can earn more points by using them more often. But if you are borrowing money that is more than your means to pay, then you will only put yourself into debt.

Sure, credit card perks are cool and attractive. But they are also often out of your league. Therefore, you need to practice mindfulness in every purchase decision you make unless you want to have your heart — I mean, bank account — broken.

9. Debit is always better than credit

This is not always the case. Yes, cash is better for when you are paying certain HP and MP1 expenses like your day-to-day needs. We also discussed earlier that a cash-only basis can actually help you develop a better budgeting habit. But credit is more preferable when you are purchasing big-ticket items, even when you have the cash to pay for them. You will be able to take advantage of available credit card perks which can include insurance, extended warranties, and cash back. Plus, using your credit card will actually improve your credit score assuming that you pay your bills on time. By using your card wisely, you can get a better credit card agreement to experience more perks and better rewards.

10. Quitting cold turkey on bad financial habits

I have said it before, you cannot change your bad financial habits all at once. It takes persistence and a sincere desire to achieve financial freedom in the long run to be able to start making changes. In fact, quitting cold turkey on all of them at once will only make your cravings and impulses worse.

If you are just beginning this journey, don't be too restrictive in how you set your monthly budget. Make room for MP2 and LP expenses, and then slowly decrease this portion of your budget as you become more comfortable with your new habits. If you are able to resist impulses or save more than what you expected, celebrate your successes by giving yourself room to enjoy and have fun.

Aside from these money myths, here are some bad financial habits that you need to break:

- Stop sacrificing your budget for convenience. Do you really have to take an Uber or is there a cheaper way to commute to where you are going? Maybe you can walk or ride a bike instead. At the same time, do you really have to Postmates your meal or can you pick up the order yourself? Better yet, buy ingredients at the grocery store and cook your meals at home. These conveniences may seem like they're a normal part of how people live their lives today. But you don't actually need them, do you? I'm not saying that you can't take an Uber or have food delivered via Postmates anymore, but you should definitely cut back on these if you need more room in your budget. This is part of learning how to prioritize in allocating your resources.

- Cut back on personal vices for the sake of your finances and, more importantly, your health. Cigarettes and alcohol may not seem like they cost a lot, but they can really add up in the long run. (Remember our Starbucks example earlier?) This tip does not just apply to smoking and drinking. Gambling can be a problem for some people too. Always eating takeout, hoarding makeup and skincare products, and your sparkling water obsession are some less obvious examples of vices.
- Do not travel without an itinerary. When you go on a holiday, try to plan your activities ahead of time. Accounting for each hour of your vacation will prevent you from going over the budget that you have set for the trip. This does not mean that you can't be spontaneous while visiting a new place. But it's always a good thing to have an idea of how you will be spending money and how much cash you need to bring with you so you do not burn your budget before the trip is even over.

Hopefully, this section has debunked some of the wrong financial habits and myths that you thought were okay or true. As you form a better attitude towards money, you will realize that these misconceptions are actually hurting your long-term financial goals. You may have been victim to these dangerous money myths and habits in the past, but you still have time to unsubscribe from these false beliefs. Start by reshaping your perspective and your actions will soon follow.

MAKING CREDIT CARDS WORK FOR YOU: HOW TO TURN YOUR CREDIT CARD INTO A GOLD MINE

Although I've been telling you to avoid using your credit card (or acquiring any kind of debt for that matter), I know that some transactions will still require it. I also know that not all debts are bad. In fact, credit card companies use your credit history, your previous debts and how diligent you are in paying them, to determine whether you have good credit score.

In this section of the book, we will discuss how you can turn your credit card into a gold mine. I will teach you the most important dos and don'ts of using your credit card. In the end, you will have a better understanding of how to properly manage your credit as well as how you can use it to your advantage.

The Dos and Don'ts of Credit Cards

Whether you are a new cardholder or a veteran in swiping, these four dos and don'ts will be your guide in making better financial decisions in terms of credit.

Do pay your balance in full and on time

In the United States, the current overall credit card debt is $807 billion, which is a $43 billion increase from last year. To put the problem in perspective, the latest available data shows that the average annual household income in the country was $60,366 while the average credit card debt was $5,884 in 2017 (Experian, 2019; Department of Numbers, 2017). This means that the average credit card debt makes about 9.74% of the average annual household income.

Like I mentioned earlier, the easiest way to get deeper into debt is to fail to pay your credit card balance on time. Most, if not all, credits cards have monthly compounded interest rates. Let's say that your credit card balance is $100 on a 7% interest rate. If you fail to pay that amount for six months, your new balance will become $642!

To maintain a good credit score and to avoid getting into unmanageable debt, you should pay your balance in full and on time. If you are trying to balance your budget between multiple credit card bills, you should implement the scheme that I mentioned in Chapter 1. Pay all the minimum balances and then use the rest of your funds to pay the debt with the highest interest rate. Once that debt is completely paid off, move on to the one with the next highest interest rate and so on.

Don't borrow beyond your means

Like spending, you should borrow money in proportion to your income. When you use your credit card, consider the installments that you will be paying. Will you be able to make each payment on time without breaking your budget? If so, then you can go ahead and use your credit card. If not, save a little more and wait until you have enough funds before making the purchase.

Don't use multiple credit cards

As much as possible, just use one credit card when making transactions. This prevents you from splitting the cost of one transaction into multiple cards. Even though each card will have a smaller balance than if you used a single card, you will still be paying the same amount at the end of the day. Let me show you what I mean.

For this example, let's say you are buying a $500 item and you have five credit cards to split the cost evenly. This means that each card will be charged $100. The minimum payment is usually 1% of your balance, but let's say that you want to pay $10 every month until you have paid off the entire amount. With a 7% interest on each card, your payment scheme will look like this:

Month
Payment
Balance
Month 0
0
$100.00
Month 1
$10
$90.00
Month 2
$10
$86.3
Month 3
$10
$82.34
...
...
...
Month 14
$10
$15.47
Month 15
$10
$6.56
Month 16
$7.02 ($6.56 + 7%)
0

You will need to pay $10 for 15 months for each card plus $7.02 in the last month, which is $785.10 in total if you are paying all cards at once. On the other hand, if you charged

$500 to one card and paid $50 per month, your payment scheme will look like this:

Month
Payment
Balance
Month 0
0
$500.00
Month 1
$50
$450.00
Month 2
$50
$431.50
Month 3
$50
$411.70
...
...
...
Month 14
$50
$77.39
Month 15
$50
$32.81
Month 16
$35.11 ($32.81 + 7%)
0

By using one card for the entire transaction, you will have to pay $50 for 15 months plus $35.11 in the last month. That's $785.11 in total.

Now, you might be thinking: "What if one card has a

smaller interest rate? Wouldn't it be smarter to split the cost with that?"

No. Just use the card with the smallest interest rate to pay for the transaction. Going back to our example, if you have another credit card with a 5% interest rate, then charge the whole $500 amount to that card. It really does not make any sense to use the other credit cards with higher interest rates because that will just drive up the total amount that you have to pay.

In addition, splitting a transaction between different cards will tempt you to pay one card at a time. Even though you consistently and punctually pay the bill for that one card, your debt will still be much bigger. That's because, while you are paying it off, the balances in the other cards will keep growing given their interest rates.

Don't max out your credit card

Credit card companies will check your gross annual income level and current credit score to determine your maximum limit. Therefore, everyone's limit is different.

But most people who reach their monthly credit limit are unable to pay off their balances, and there's a pretty obvious reason as to why. If a person is capable of paying off their credit card limit, they will be making the transaction with either cash or a debit card. The fact is most of these people who are maxing out their credit cards are not making good financial decisions. They splurge on non-essential items, cave to impulse-buying behaviors, and use their credit cards to support these wants.

As a general rule, do not max out your credit card. If you are unable to pay off a huge balance, your credit score and whole financial status will suffer. The optimal balance is 30% of your credit limit or below. Try to stay within this range so you do not put yourself at risk.

Using Your Credit Card to Your Advantage

There are several ways to use your credit card to your

advantage. First of all, you should treat it as a supplementary tool to your budget, i.e., you can use it in accordance to the budget that you created in the first chapter. This way, you can earn points and rewards without worrying about going over budget or getting into debt.

To stay on track of how much you have spent, use your credit card provider's online or mobile banking system. Here, you can find your statement, balance, minimum monthly payments, and due dates in real time.

You should also save the majority of your credit card limit for big-ticket items such as new furniture for your home or plane tickets for a holiday trip. Compared to buying smaller items with cheaper price tags, it will be easier to remember that you used your credit card and should therefore make payments.

In the same context, try to avoid using your credit card unless you need to make an important purchase. Throughout this book, this has been the most common tip I have given you: Always prioritize when it comes to spending. If you need to buy, say, a new laundry unit, maybe you should not use your credit card for a plane ticket for now, especially if you can't sustain the pace of paying the total due amount per month. Remember that your credit card charges interest. The total amount you pay will increase over time if you are unable to keep up with monthly payments for these two items.

Lastly, take advantage of the rewards. Credit card providers usually offer a wide range of perks including cash back, frequent flyer miles, and discounts from select and partner stores. However, be careful about getting hooked on these rewards. If you are spending way too much just to obtain one of these bonuses, you are making bad financial decisions. Always be a smart consumer.

HOW TO MAKE MONEY ONLINE: IS DROP-SHIPPING A GOOD OPTION?

The internet has been integral in globalization and the opening of new markets that didn't exist some 10 to 20 years ago. Advances in technology, especially in how we use the internet, has led to some viable business opportunities that can help you earn a substantial amount of money on the side. In fact, you can make an online business your primary source of income once you have established yourself as a reliable supplier of goods and services that your niche is looking for.

Drop-shipping, for example, has become increasingly popular as a startup venture in recent years. In this section of the book, we will primarily discuss drop-shipping as a business model. You will learn about how it works as well as how you can benefit from it as an entrepreneur.

In addition, I will also give you a few business ideas for online entrepreneurship. This section will be all about making money on the internet, whether you want it to be your primary or supplementary source of income, which can help you further build your wealth. Hopefully, by the end of this section, you will get inspired to start your own online business.

Drop-shipping Business

Drop-shipping is an e-commerce business model that aspiring entrepreneurs have been particularly interested in. There's a simple explanation for this. See, when you enter this type of business, you will most likely not be selling your own products to customers. Instead, you become the middleman between the customer and the drop-shipping supplier. The customer will order items from your online store, but the drop-shipping supplier is in charge of picking up, packing up, and delivering the order.

On the other side of things, the drop-shipping supplier partners with businesses who want to expand their reach.

The brand will sell its products to the drop-shipping supplier who will keep them in storage until a customer orders them from your website.

In simpler terms, the drop-shipping business model involves the following processes:

1. Different brands sell their products to a drop-shipping supplier.
2. Customers order products from the brands through your website.
3. You forward the order details and shipping information to the drop-shipping supplier.
4. The drop-shipping supplier will process the order and ship it out on behalf of your store.
5. You earn the difference between the price of the product on your website and how much the drop-shipping supplier charges you.

Because drop-shipping suppliers usually buy products from brands in bulk, they get the items in wholesale price (or in even bigger discounts) instead of retail. This is how you are able to offer the retail price on your website. In some cases, you may even be able to offer more competitive prices than those in other places.

It is true that there are many benefits to adopting a drop-shipping business model, especially if you are just beginning to establish a business. However, it also has its own set of disadvantages. As an entrepreneur, you need to have a more holistic understanding of what drop-shipping is. So let's talk about the pros and cons of this business model before you decide if it's the right income-generating venture for you.

Pros of Drop-shipping

The first and most attractive benefit of the drop-shipping business model is its simplicity. As a new entrepreneur, you can start operating a business in three easy steps. First, you should find a good drop-shipping supplier. Next, you have to open your online store. Create your website and use social media to generate buzz and to start a following that you can turn into paying customers. The last thing left to do is to start accepting orders.

There is practically no startup cost in starting this online business. You will have to pay for your website's domain name and hosting fees, but that's it. You do not need to find a warehouse or to open a physical store, which means you do not have to pay for rent and other associated costs. You also will not have to buy or manufacture your initial inventory. Plus, with so many drop-shipping suppliers selling a wide range of products, you have a lot of options when it comes to what kind of online store you want to establish. Fashion and beauty? Home improvement and decor? Technology? The choice is up to you.

Because you do not have a physical store, you will not have to pay for manpower (i.e., storekeeper, manager, etc.), utilities (like water, electricity, and office supplies), and other costs relating to operations. You may have to purchase additional apps that can help your website run smoother and become more user friendly, but the cost of that does not come close to how much you will have to spend if you open a traditional business.

As you can tell, you will have significantly less costs in operating your business if you choose a drop-shipping model. Therefore, the return on investment is likely to be much faster if you do everything right. You also have significantly less risks; if you do not meet your target sales, you do not lose any money because you did not put money out in the first place. On the other hand, if you open a physical store, you need to meet a certain number of sales in order to break even all of your fixed costs.

Lastly, one of the greatest benefits of a drop-shipping model is that you can run your business from anywhere. You are not tethered to a location, which gives you a lot of flexibility. As long as you have a strong and stable internet connection and your laptop with you, you can make profits wherever you may be. You also get to control your time; you are your own boss.

Cons of Drop-shipping

In whatever type of business, there are always risks involved especially in the beginning. The drop-shipping model, as I mentioned earlier, is like any other business; it has its own set of disadvantages that you need to consider. Although the benefits above look promising, you have to look at both sides of the coin before you hop on board with this business idea.

The first disadvantage of drop-shipping that I and so many other business-minded people see is control. Even though you get to decide where and when you work, you have little control over the quality of the product before, during, and after it has been shipped. So many problems can arise during the packaging and shipping of the product. Items may get mishandled and broken. Wrong items can be packaged in the order. Problems in shipping can cause late deliveries. Even if you did not create the product or handle the shipment yourself, it is still your online store that will receive negative feedback. This is why you need to find a good drop-shipping supplier before you open your store. Even so, there are no guarantees that these problems will not occur.

With a drop-shipping model, you will also not be able to manage the inventory as efficiently as may you want to. Because products are stored in the drop-shipping supplier's warehouse, you often do not have a real time accounting of each item. The drop-shipping supplier is supposed to inform you about changes in inventory, but there can be problems in communication. For instance, the information can be delayed, and a customer might order a sold out or unavailable product from your website before you are able to update its status. Today, there are software updates that allow you to see changes in inventory in real time, but those usually come at an additional cost depending on who your drop-shipping supplier is.

In addition, drop-shipping is currently a very competitive market. Like I said earlier, a lot of startup entrepreneurs are getting in on the action. This is understandable given the attractive benefits of drop-shipping. However, with this level of competition, you may find it harder to stay on top of search engine results. Unless you want to focus on a specific niche or have formed a strong social media presence, it will be challenging to get organic traffic into your website during the first several months of business.

I believe that the last notable disadvantage of drop-shipping is its comparatively lower profit margin. A drop-shipping supplier will be able to get products from brands at the lowest possible price. However, they will not be charging you by that minimum because they are also a business that needs to make money. Therefore, if you partner up with a drop-shipping supplier, you should expect lower profits than if you purchase inventory directly from a brand, a manufacturer, or a wholesaler. However, doing the latter will technically change your business model, so you can't say that you are running a drop-shipping website anymore.

Should you try drop-shipping?

The truth is that I can't give you a straight answer. I do not know for certain if you will succeed as a drop-shipping website. It is up to you to weigh the pros and cons. At the end of the day, the real reason a business becomes successful is because of the passion and drive of the people behind it. Without hard work and zeal in entrepreneurship, a person will never be able to build a thriving business.

So ask yourself this: Are you willing to do whatever it takes? If you are serious about putting in time and effort, you will find a way to make this type of business successful even if you are entering such a competitive market.

Online Business Opportunities

For those who are not interested in drop-shipping, here are a few online business ideas that can inspire you to start your own entrepreneurial journey.

1. Airbnb

Do you have a spare room? Maybe you have another property. If you work overseas, your permanent residence may be collecting dust at the moment. Instead of letting this real estate stand stagnantly, make some passive income by opening an Airbnb.

The average income of Airbnb hosts varies by location, amenities, and the number of guests you can accommodate per booking. However, you can receive payment within 24 hours of guests checking in. You can also earn more when you become an Airbnb superhost, so make sure to keep your place clean and accommodating.

2. Etsy Store

For artists who like to create Bespoke and handmade items, you can start an Etsy store to sell your creations. I know people who started their businesses on Etsy and then later opened physical stores that carry the same items that their customers on the website have loved.

Before you set up shop, however, you need to learn about the different fees involved in running your own Etsy store.

For instance, the website charges a $0.20 listing fee for every item that you're selling. To help minimize this cost, start with a small collection of items and then produce several copies of each item. Let's say you're selling posters on Etsy. You can list 5 designs and then print 20 copies of each design so you're only paying $1 for 100 products.

Aside from the listing fee, Etsy also charges a sales commission of 5% for every item you sell. There is also a payment processing fee, which is 3% of the price of an item plus $0.25 for credit card transactions. Meanwhile, PayPal charges a 2.9% plus $0.30 payment processing fee. When deciding on how much to price your items, take these fees into consideration.

3. Instagram Niche Store

Instagram has introduced a Shop feature recently that allows businesses to tag their products on posts. This marketing feature is supposed to help established brands advertise their products on the website which only proves how this social media platform has become a lucrative place of business online. If you already have an online store, you can use the Shop feature to market your merchandise.

Alternatively, you can sell products directly from Instagram by opening a niche store. I have been seeing this trend for quite a while now; small-scale entrepreneurs use this social networking site as a launching pad for their online businesses. Stay-at-home moms, students, and even young professionals open their own niche stores to make extra income. They sell beauty products, pre-loved items, phone and laptop cases, imported goods, and much more. From where I stand, I think that it is actually a pretty genius idea to utilize Instagram for money-making ventures.

Except for creating or buying your initial inventory, there is virtually no other cost to opening an Instagram niche store. You can operate the business from the comforts of your own home. Just make an Instagram account for your business and you can easily start selling products by posting pictures of them 0n the app.

Before you accept orders though, make sure that you have a payment and shipping structure in place. Speaking of which, one of the challenges of operating your own Instagram niche store is how you would ship your products to your customers. So find a reliable courier that can pick up and deliver packages on time.

4. Blogging/Vlogging

I am grouping these two business opportunities, though they are vastly different, simply because they have the same underlying concept: You are selling yourself as a brand when you start a blog or vlog. Let me explain further.

Blogging primarily involves publishing written content on a niche of topics on your website. Most bloggers present themselves as experts (or at least knowledgeable) on their selected niche and offer advice to their audience. For example, if you master the tips I have shared with you on this book, you can perhaps start a blog centered on personal financial management. You can document the steps you take to change your spending habits and budgeting style. By sharing your experiences, you can help other people become better at handling their finances.

You can earn money as a blogger through banner and strip advertisements. You can also join Amazon's associate program to earn real dollars. At the same time, when you have an established blog, brands may reach out to you for sponsorships. You may also get invited to speaking engagements that expose you to a wider audience, which means more traffic to your website. The more successful your blog is, the more opportunities will open for you, and the more possibilities to make it grow as a business.

Meanwhile, vlogging or video blogging is a growing industry on YouTube. Social media influencers and even mainstream celebrities create their own channels on the website. It used to be that earning money on YouTube was an added bonus to having a platform to create videos. However, vlogging has become a lucrative source of income as much as it is a venue to share one's talents and interests.

Vlogging is a highly competitive industry given how saturated YouTube is today. However, if you manage to build a substantial audience, the rewards are extraordinary. You can earn money through advertisements, brand deals, and selling your own merchandise. These income-generating opportunities also spill over to your other social media accounts. Brands may reach out and ask you to post about their products on, say, your Instagram and Twitter profiles. And for the most successful YouTube personalities, the mainstream media also opens its doors to give them new opportunities.

For example, Lilly Singh is one of the oldest creators on the platform in terms of when she launched her YouTube channel. She has recently signed a deal with NBC to host her own late night show which makes her the first queer woman of color to become a talk show host (Moniuszko, 2019). David Dobrik is also a popular YouTuber who started out as a creator on Vine. His success in creating videos has landed him a hosting gig at the 2019 Teen Choice Awards (Baumgartner, 2019).

Vlogging can catapult you into celebrity status, but it is not an easy path towards the top. If you have a passion for creating videos though, you should definitely give it a try.

5. Freelancing Jobs

If you have a skill set that you think other people may be looking to outsource, try freelancing. You can choose to do it part-time or full-time; although, more and more people are deciding to make it their main source of income. There are a lot of freelancing websites where you can find clients to work with. But three of the most popular websites among freelancers today include Fiverrr, UpWork, and Reddit.

Did you learn anything from this chapter that will help you effectively build your wealth? I sure hope so! But whether you're planning to start an online business or invest in stocks and bonds, always remember to make financial decisions that will propel you towards your long-term goals and help you in achieving financial freedom.

AFTERWORD

There have been common themes throughout this book that I have reiterated from time to time. But let me sum up in one word the most important lesson that you can take away from everything I have shared with you in this book: Prioritize.

In every financial decision, the key is to prioritize. Manage your resources in a way that benefits you in the long run, puts your necessities first, and gives you more time to spend with your family. The techniques that I have taught you in this book were meant to instill this fundamental lesson in your mind.

Let's go back to the metaphor that I used at the beginning of this book. In the construction of a house, what do builders prioritize? Do they put up the walls first? Build the roof? Lay down the flooring? Paint? Furnish?

No. They build the foundation first. They pour the concrete and make sure that it's level. They let it dry before they build a house on top of it. Then, they build the frame of the house before putting up walls, building the roof, installing windows and doors, etc. There is a process that needs to be followed for the house to be livable. If the engineer of the house ignored problems in its construction, the house will collapse sooner or later no matter how good the finished product looks.

Financial management is a lot similar to building a house. You need to go through the process in order to change your overall attitude towards money. You can't just start a business to earn income to pay your debts. At the same time, you can't achieve financial freedom without addressing the money problems that you currently have.

Hopefully, the techniques I have shared with you will help you to prioritize. Let's have a quick recap of how you can effectively implement these techniques in your life.

No matter how financially stable (or unstable) you are at the moment, there are two ways you can categorize your priorities: time and importance. We discussed these on the very first section of the book (Different Budgeting Types: Which Ones DO Work and Which DON'T), which should make you understand just how important building the foundation is.

Anyway, let's look at each category.

Time: Always prioritize long-term financial goals over short-term financial goals.

Let's say that you are a college student and that your long-term goal is to graduate on time because this allows you to find a stable, high-paying job. Your short-term goal is to earn money while you study, so you have additional allowance.

During a particularly hectic week when you have multiple tests lined up, your manager asks you to work longer shifts. Now you're faced with two options: Do you agree to take longer shifts, so you can earn extra cash, or do you decline, so you can have time to study?

The answer is obvious, right? Choose the latter. You can always earn the additional income that you would have earned if you did longer shifts. But the time you would have sacrificed could be detrimental to your test scores and GPA.

Opportunities like this will always present themselves to you. You just have to keep your eyes on your long-term goals and not allow short-term goals distract you along the way.

Importance: Always prioritize your needs over your wants.

This tip isn't just applicable to budgeting; you can also use it when making other financial decisions. For example, let's say that all of your peers have started to invest in real estate. They're purchasing homes in the suburbs to settle in. You, on the other hand, still live in a one-bedroom apartment in the city.

Your close friend tells you that there's a beautiful home on their street that's being sold below market value. Just for fun, you check it out to see what it has to offer. You realize that the house is in good condition and requires little improvements. Do you make an offer?

Buying a home is a big commitment. Although this house checks off a lot of the items on your bucket list, it might not be the best time for you to invest in real estate. Maybe you're still paying off debts. Maybe you're not stable enough to pay the down payment on this house. Maybe your current place of residence is close enough to work that you don't have to pay for gas or spend a substantial amount of time commuting.

On initial thought, you may want to buy this house. But it's possible that it isn't what you need right now.

It's also essential that you look at the intersection of time and importance. Once you have mastered this important skill, you will find that a lot of your financial woes are easier to solve.

Before you close this book, I want to congratulate you on taking the first step towards financial freedom. By reaching this point, you have proven to yourself that you are ready to make the necessary changes in order to achieve your goals. However, learning the techniques is different from actually implementing them. As you turn this last page, you should carry everything you have learned but face the new chapter — your journey towards financial freedom — with grace. You may stumble and fall once in a while, but you can always come back to this book to remind yourself of why you're saving, investing, and changing your spending habits. With persistence, you can achieve your financial objectives and live your dream life at any age. There's no doubt about that.

REAL ESTATE INVESTING:

HOW TO DOUBLE THE VALUE OF YOUR HOME - FOR LITTLE OR EVEN NO MONEY!

INTRODUCTION

Increasing the value of your home should be on any real estate investor's radar. Whether it's your primary residence, or a home you've bought to flip, or the increasingly popular "live and flip" lifestyle - it's a no brainer, and an essential component to building huge wealth for you and your family.

The average American now spends 33% of their income on housing expenditures. So, by making smart decisions regarding real estate, you can cut that number in half. That represents real money in your pocket, not tiny gains made by skipping Starbucks or making your own packed lunch.

Gone are the days where people bought a home at 22 and proceeded to live in it for their entire lives. Now more than ever, re-sale price should be at the forefront of your mind when it comes to carrying out home renovations.

But, it's tough to know which renovations are worth it. Will you make your money back?

However, what 90% of amateur real estate investors don't know is that there are a ton of ways you can increase the value of your home for little money, or even FOR FREE!

It pays to get it right when it comes to renovations. So, before you paint the living room hot pink, drop 10 large on a brand new steam room, or spend $5,000 on a full garden remodelling - take a look at these handy tips.

Beyond renovations, when it comes time to sell your home, there are a number of steps you can take to give yourself a huge advantage, and maximize your profits - even in a bad market!

I hope you learn a lot from this book, and I hope you make a lot of money with real estate going forward.

26 WAYS TO INCREASE FINAL SALE PRICE FOR LITTLE OR EVEN NO MONEY AT ALL!

Use these low cost, and even free tips to add significant amounts to the final sale price of your home.

Clean up outside

Studies have shown that litter outside can decrease your home value by up to 12%. This goes to show that even something tiny, and technically outside of your control - can negatively affect your home in a huge way.

Get the garden in order

You've sorted out the front, now it's time to deal with the back. Grab those weeds and get them out of there as soon as possible. Fire up the hedge trimmer and keep everything neat and tidy. Even a $2 pot of heather by your front door can give a warm, welcoming appeal to any guest or home viewer.

. . .

Ditch the novelty door knob

You never get a second chance to make a first impression, and that's no less true than in home buying and selling. I'm sure your love of cats or pumpkins is completely justified, but remember not everyone shares the same tastes. Neutral may be boring, but remember your door, mailbox and letterbox are among the first things people see when they come to view your home.

Homeowners have reported up to a 5% increase in offer just after changing from a novelty door knob or a more traditional one.

The same goes if you're stuck with a large, uninviting steel door. You can easily add wood grain to make it look nicer, and if you're looking for a cheaper option - just paint it.

Get some brand new stainless steel house numbers as well, at just $5-10 each they're well worth the investment.

The novelty doormat can go as well, "Welcome, bitches" and "Owner is shady, dogs are cool" may not be to everyone's taste…

Upgrade your light fixtures

Another fairly cheap improvement is upgraded lighting, especially for your kitchen. Get rid of the dull, recessed lights in the kitchen and opt for an inexpensive - but nice looking chandelier instead. You can get some really great traditional and modern designs for as little as $100 online.

. . .

Paint your way to profits

A gallon of good quality paint costs around $25 on average. Once again, neutral colors work best and have the widest appeal, so maybe keep the military greens and cotton candy pinks on the shelf for another day.

If you're going to pick just one room to paint, make it the kitchen or living room - as these have a greater "first impression" appeal than the master bedroom.

One thing to note about kitchen colors is that white doesn't work. Design experts at Zillow Digs found that homes with all white kitchens sold for $1,400 less than equivalent ones with kitchens of over light hues.

If your budget allows for it, do an external repainting. Nothing says "I could lowball these guys" than an outdated external paintjob. So if your home is looking faded, painting is a great way to bring your value up to where it should be. Remember to keep colors consistent with the rest of your neighborhood - no one wants to live in "the pink house".

Pro tip: If you go to Home Depot, Lowes, Ace Hardware or any other large home improvement store, you can often find near-full pots of paint for up to 50% off. This is known as the "oops" paint, where buyers have returned the pot after realising they didn't like the color. The best part is, you can often find these in multiple pots so if you have a large painting job you can save hundreds of dollars this way.

. . .

Popcorn Ceilings

Remember when popcorn ceilings were in? Me neither - but many houses still have them. If yours suffers from this unfortunate affliction, get rid of them ASAP.

WHILE THIS PROCESS IS FAIRLY LABOR INTENSIVE, IT'S ALSO EXTREMELY CHEAP TO SORT OUT YOURSELF. MAKE SURE YOU COMPLETELY COVER ALL FURNITURE BEFORE YOU BEGIN.

MORE TIPS

Putting in a pool will drown your home value
Everyone loves a pool right? Wrong.

Many low-maintenance types don't want to deal with the hassle of having to constantly maintain a pool year-round, especially in areas where it's not usable for all 12 months.

If it's broke - definitely do fix it
You'd be surprised just how much minor (and cheap) cosmetic renovations can have a positive overall effect on your home value. Fixing broken roof tiles and cleaning the gutters are just two of the many things you can do in half a day which can easily increase home value by 1 or 2%. Remember, minor edges like this are what sets professionals apart from amateurs in the real estate market.

Install a new showerhead
Remember the 5 star hotel experience you want to provide? Well all 5 star hotels have great showers, and particularly, great showerheads. This is a simple job you can do yourself and often involves nothing more than using pliers

or a wrench to remove your old shower head then repeat the process in reverse for a new one.

Although luxury models can cost upwards of $1,000, you can get good mid-range rain style showerheads for as little as $200 at Home Depot.

Bedrooms bring profits

Converting a bedroom into a home gym, studio or wine cellar may appeal to some, but to most buyers the more bedrooms the better.

This doubles down when you start installing semi-permanent items like specialist refrigerators and bookshelves that the new owner will have to spend money to gut and get rid of. So if you are going to convert one, with the view to moving out in a few years, ensure the features are easy to return to their natural state.

So remember this, if you have a three-bedroom house with a den, the only reason the den can't be considered a bedroom may be because it doesn't have a closet. If you add a closet to that room, you've now got a four-bedroom house - it's just that simple.

For the price of an Ikea closet, you can have an entire extra bedroom in your house.

Garages are for cars

Following on from the bedroom conversion point. Garages converted to play rooms or home gyms are far less valuable to a garage to it used for its intended function - to store cars. Buyers want to keep their cars out of the rain and snow and have a space to store all their outdoor gear.

Note for my UK readers: The opposite is true across the pond. With the rise of off-street parking with larger driveways, 90% of British garages don't contain a car - so removing you garage and adding extra living space may well pay off. It costs around £10,000 to remove your garage and you can calculate your rough ROI by multiplying square footage gained by local price per square foot.

Ask your realtor

An often overlooked area - no one does this, and I really don't know why. Simply ask your realtor what kind of features people are looking for when they buy a house in your area, then add them. That way you don't have to try and predict what people will like, and more importantly won't have to rely on your own imagination.

MORE TIPS

Kit out your kitchen

You can absolutely do this on the cheap - so you don't need to go hunting for the marble catalogue anytime soon. Even basic cosmetic upgrades like replacing the faucets, cabinet door handles and lighting fixtures can have a dramatically positive effect.

If you can't afford to replace things, just give them a coat of paint - even this gives your kitchen an extra boost.

The kitchen is still very much the heart and soul of the home. It's where everyone congregates at parties and it's where most of that "accidental" family time (that people value the most) occurs - and more importantly, it's where buyers and realtors make a beeline for in houses they know will fetch a high price.

Little fixes like energy efficient lightbulbs, a nice floral centerpiece for a viewing can really put a potential buyer in a good mood, and drive up their own perceived value of the home.

Having cohesive appliances is another value booster.

You may have read the dishwasher bullet point in the Amazon description for this book. Well, here's the secret revealed by a customer service representative of a major manufacturer.

Many dishwasher panels are white on one side and black on the other. So if yours doesn't match, you may be able to just flip it around so it does!

All you have to do is unscrew two screws, slide out the panel and flip it around. Sure enough you have a black (or white) panel to match your other appliances.

(Don't) Look down

I hate to break it to your but your floor is probably gross. Especially if it's more than 10 years old. Old, scruffy carpet isn't doing anyone any favors. Plus, flooring is one of the first thing buyers notice when they enter a property.

It's not a case of hardwood vs. carpet - it's a case of clean and new vs. dirty and old. No matter what kind of flooring you have, make sure it's clean. If you have a few hundred dollars spare I'd recommend getting your carpet deep cleaned by a pro.

Replacing the carpet is usually a poor investment as this is often one of the first improvements buyers make when purchasing a home. Cleaning gives you much more bang for your buck.

Energy Efficient Appliances

Buyers are always looking for ways to save money on their future purchase, and energy efficient appliances are a great way to do this. But the trick to buying these appliances (this is especially true if you live in the house you're planning to sell) is to buy new appliances *before* the old ones break.

There are actually better months to buy appliances as well. September and October are generally when manufacturers release the latest models, so this is when old models will be discounted in order to get them off the shop floor/out of the warehouse to make room for the new ones.

If you want to double down, and wait for a potentially killer deal - January may well be your best bet. Even some of the older models will be out of stock by this time, the ones that remain will be discounted even further.

There are a few exceptions to this rule, as May is the best time to snag a bargain on refrigerators. Manufacturers want to get the new models out before summer.

Can you guess when air conditioners are at their cheapest? That's right, between October and February when the demand for them is at its lowest point.

If you're looking for a second hand appliance, you may be able to get an even better deal. Appliances are similar to cars in that they lose approximately 50% of their value as soon as they leave the store. So you can get some amazing deals on barely used, top of the line items if you check sites like Craigslist. Check out your local refurbishing center as well.

Security features

If you're in an area populated by young couples and young families, security features are especially important. Safety and security of their kids is every parents number one concern. Having basic security systems installed in your home is an easy way to ramp up the final sale price.

On the lower end of things, roller shutters on your window might well be worth looking into.

Ironically, the alarm industry itself has long been full of sketchy characters who sell on fear or prey on the elderly. It's often tough to decide exactly how much you should spend on your alarm setup. Luckily, since the rise of the internet, and the availability of good information, it's never been easier to install your own device.

Systems will built-in smartphones apps are increasingly common these days, and you may want to spring for one with these features if you plan to sell your home anytime soon.

Avoid systems with a extremely low initial set-up cost which is then destroyed by high monthly monitoring fees.

For just a few hundred dollars you can get a complete setup, with zero monthly fees

Wireless system have much greater resale value as the lack of wiring is one less thing for a new homeowner to deal with.

Additionally, It's not uncommon for homes to have CCTV cameras these days - and they are far less expensive than you think. You can install a camera yourself for as little as $100 and this could increase your overall home value by up to 5%.

One word of caution, in some states it is illegal for your camera to record a part of anyone else's property. Double check your camera angles before finalizing an installation, and consider informing your neighbors of your plan to install cameras. After all, your neighbor is someone you always want to maintain a positive relationship with.

Your sink is the most important appliance

That's right, not your stove, not your dishwasher - your sink. If you have the extra cash, install a farmhouse sink. A study by home appraisal service Zillow found that home listed with a farmhouse sink sold for 8% above their value and 53 days sooner than similar homes that had regular sinks. These don't have to cost the Earth either, for under 200 dollars you can install one yourself, while keeping your current plumbing setup.

The million dollar fence question

What kind of fence should you have? White picket? High enough to keep prying eyes away? The only correct answer is a freshly painted one. Get 10L of fence paint for $50 and go to town. A freshly painted fence gives off the sense that your home is well maintained and it's one less thing for a potential buyer to worry about.

Hire a professional cleaning crew

This may be the single biggest piece of advice in this entire book. If you only have a few hundred dollars to spare on renovations, the best use of your money is to hire a full cleaning crew and let them loose in your home. Make sure absolutely everything is covered, having a spotless home will give visitors an impression of calm and relaxation.

People are visual creatures, and they want to visualize what their ideal home will look like, and believe me, no one's ideal home has dirty countertops or carpets. By presenting an image that pleases them, they're going to want to spend more money their potential new home.

MORE TIPS

The $75 curb appeal trick

"Curb appeal" is one of those things every realtor talks about. It's vital you make sure your house gives a good first impression. An often overlooked area of this is your driveway. Luckily, you can rent a power washer from as little as $75/day and make your driveway look good as new. Go crazy with the thing and do your sidewalks (and your neighbor's), outside deck and exterior siding. As an added bonus, power washers are incredibly fun to use, and probably the closet you'll ever come to feeling like Sylvester Stallone in Rambo.

Tapping into the lucrative Chinese home buyer market

Chinese overseas property investment has increased by a factor of 20 in the previous 10 years. Chinese citizens are projected to spend over $20 billion on property in 2017 alone, and if you live in a particularly affluent area (especially on the West coast), you may be part of their target market. But what you may not know about the Chinese is that they don't use toilet paper in their bathrooms. Instead they have a bidet (or bum-gun for those of you into less formal terminology).

What may surprise you is that installing one of these requires no additional plumbing, will save you money on toilet paper that it'll pay for itself within a year. AND, has huge appeal when selling to any portion of the Asian market, but especially the Chinese - who like to feel at home as soon as they enter a house.

The $1 quick fix guaranteed to bring hundreds back in return

Outlets get dirty really quick, especially white ones. But you can buy new outlet plates for $1 each, bam - brand spanking new outlet plates that give you house that extra clean touch. You can even go the extra mile and paint them to be the same color as your walls.

One addition point to make on this is the importance of consistency. Don't just replace one or two outlets, replace them all. People like consistency and regularity. Things one odd colored outlet covers can subconsciously throw off buyers without them even realizing it.

Ditch the family photos

The old marketing adage "nobody cares about you, they only care about themselves" rings true here. People want to picture themselves in their poential new home, which also happens to be your current home. That's hard if there's 50 photos of you, your kids, your kids and Auntie Marge, your kids and Auntie Marge and her pet ferret Rollie etc.

This is where the concept of depersonalization comes in. If there's one thing 5 star hotels all have in common, it's that they are *not* personal. They are a soothing space, even somewhat neutral - a blank canvas if you will. How does this relate to your home? Well, a few family photos here and there is perfectly acceptable but try to keep them in standing photo frames rather than walled ones. Your ideal look should be a luxury hotel suite rather than someone's home. Remember, no one wants to walk into a hotel room that the maid hasn't cleaned yet. As a knock-on effect, you're going to be moving anyway so why not start the packing process earlier and save yourself a headache going forward?

De-Clutter, De-clutter, De-clutter

This obvious tip is often overlooked by those who believe their home isn't actually cluttered. Having excess stuff just laying around makes your home look smaller than it really is, while simultaneously giving the impression of a lack of storage space.

Even if you don't want to through away some of things, at the very least put them in the attic or in the garage.

Strategically placed mirrors

Instead of bulding a skylight or conservatory, add a few mirrors to give the impression of extra light. More maximum impact, hand these opposite a window - which gives the impressions that there are actually two windows.

How to save thousands when hiring contractors

It cannot be stressed enough, getting the right contractor (especially for a larger job) can save you money, time and potential headaches.

The number one rule of hiring contractors is to get multiple bids for every job - at least 3. If your roof needs replacing, get 3 roofers to come and look at it. The same for if your entire home needs re-wiring, get 3 electricians in.

These 3 bids will get you 3 different answers about your needs, you can also let them know (politely) that there are other contractors looking at the job so if they're serious, they'll be willing to go above and beyond for you.

ROOM-BY-ROOM GUIDE TO STAGING YOUR HOME

Did you know that only 10-15% of buyers can visualize your home differently than the way it looks when they walk in the door? Therefore, it's important to give them as much room for imagination as possible, and most of this revolves around keeping your house clean and removing clutter - here's a handy room by room guide to staging your house so that potential buyers get can the most out of their viewing.

THE KITCHEN:

- Remove all appliances and clutter off counters. Counters should be completely clear from any non-necessary items.
- Clean all appliances. If they really look out of date, research the cost for new ones as you may get the money back - especially for worktop ones.
- Clear out the dishes. This is the perfect time to get rid of the stuff you don't want anymore - after all you'll be moving anyway. Do you really need the

"world's best dad" coffee mug or the Tupperware that no longer has a lid? Donate anything you no longer need to Goodwill. Once you've done that - you can pack all the remaining dishes in preparation for your move. All you need to leave out is a single set of matching dishes in the cupboard, just so the buyer can see that someone does indeed live there right now and they're not visiting a showhome. This has the additional advantage of making your cupboard space look more spacious when buyers open up and take a look.

- All buyers will open your fridge (I don't know why - they just will), so be sure to clean it out and of course throw out any excess food. Ideally schedule your open houses for when you are running low on supplies, because this will allow your fridge to naturally have less items in.
- The same goes for your pantry, once again donate any items you don't need and just leave a row of nicely organized items. Once again, this is to demonstrate just how spacious your cupboard and pantry space is!
- Once you've successfully decluttered and thrown out what needs to be thrown out - you can begin the staging process. This starts with a nice centerpiece on your counter. This could be an decent sized plant (like an orchid) or a big bowl of oranges or lemons (opt for the real thing). Make sure you set the dining room table as well, don't forget the unlit candles.
- If you haven't got time to bake cookies, buy some baked goods to put out for your open house. Don't forget the essential oil diffuser either, I'll explain why later in the book

LIVING ROOM

THE LIVING ROOM:

- Remove the majority of the items from the mantelpiece or other shelving areas. You can leave up one or two family photos but the majority can be packed away ready for your move.
- Ditch the kid's artwork as well. I'm sure they're very talented, but you can save that for your new place.
- Hang generic artwork if you have any, if not just make sure the walls are clean.
- If the room needs to be painted, paint it,like I said before, it's one of the cheapest ways to maximize your finale sale price.
- Repair any light switches, loose curtain rods, etc. If it needs fixing - do it now. You'll have to fix it anyway, so before someone looks around your home is the best time.
- Make sure all the skirting boards and outlets are clean as well.

- Ditch any old magazines or newspapers on the table
- If you have extra furniture that takes away from your room, put it in storage. Ask your realtor if you really can't decide, they'll be able to make an informed judgment as to what buyers will like and won't like seeing. It' worth the extra expense because potential buyers are going to see your garage and spare room - so you want to keep those clean as well.
- Stick with one theme throughout your home. You don't need an Asian inspired kitchen next to your post-industrial living room for example. Your home should have a consistent and unified look. Plus this also helps you get rid of a lot of stuff
- Put a vase of flowers in the living room on open house day. You can put some finger food here as well, but I personally think the kitchen is always the best place for open house food.

BATHROOM

THE BATHROOM(S):

- Get out the travel toiletries bag, because you'll be living out of this while your home is on the market. Your bathroom needs to be spotless for the coming weeks.
- Clear away all the bottles and jars from any bath rack and within the shower itself. Don't forget the medicine cabinets either (home viewers will look)
- Repaint the bathroom as well, an easy return on investment.
- Do you have sliding shower doors? Are they sticking? If so replace the rollers, this doesn't cost a look and makes them look like new again.
- Fix any leaky faucets
- Get a new set of white towels for when you're showing the house, make your bathroom look like a hotel bathroom
- Place a single flower on the bathroom counter -

just something to draw viewer's eyes in when they enter the room

BEDROOMS

THE BEDROOMS:

- Remove all personal items from the dressers and bedside tables, with the exception of one, non-controversial book
- Pack away any excess clothes from your closet. If you really don't need them it's time to throw them out. Fold the rest of your clothes neatly, as if you were running a clothing store. Remember, the emptier your closet the better, give the buyer as much potential room as possible.
- Invest in new bed sheets, remember you can take these with you and it'll make the bed look much nicer for any prospective buyer. Remember - make it feel like a hotel room
- Once again, do the curtains need replacing, does the carpet need cleaning?
- Make sure your windows are clean, inside and outside.

- You can have one or two family photos but anything more will be overkill.
- If you have an additional bedroom you're currently using as a storage room, now's the time to turn it back into a bedroom again. If you were running a hotel, you wouldn't have one of the guest bedrooms as a storage closet - don't do the same in your home.

EXTERIOR

THE EXTERIOR:

We've already covered this somewhat but it should be reiterated anyway.

- Don't neglect the outside of your home - you never get a second chance to make a good first impression
- Ensure your front door has a fresh coat of paint and that both the porch light and doorbell are fully functional - you don't want to leave potential buyers waiting outside now do you?
- Add a few pops of color to the yard, and clear out any dead plants and make sure your grass to cut
- If you have an outdoor patio or dining table, set some wine glasses on that, alternatively if it's winter and you have a firepit - get that going

Final checks:

Take a photo of each room, is there anything out of place or any stains you haven't noticed. If not, then you can kick back and relax, maybe even pour yourself a glass of wine.

The hard part of over, now you just need to let your realtor do their job and your renovations will pay for themselves in your final sale price.

Bonus staging tip:

Create a welcome note for your buyers, introducing them to the neighborhood. Many buyers will be local so they'll already know much of the information, but it's useful for any out of town buyers who may be looking at the property. You can add handy tidbits like local attractions and niche interests that may be of use to a potential buyer.

THE #1 MOST OVERLOOKED FACTOR IN SELLING A HOME

*S*mell is the most powerful human sense in terms of memorability. That's why certain foods always remind us of our childhood or certain events in our life.

Unfortunately, negative smells have even more of an effect than positive ones. 41 percent of real estate pros have listed "bad smells" as part of their most expensive mistakes when it came to selling a home.

Musty odors give buyers notice that there may be an underlying mold or mildew problem in the home. Both damp carpet and wet ceiling tiles are tell-tale signs of these. While you definitely need to consult a professional if you have a major mold problem, smaller issues can be dealt with by yourself. A $200 dehumidifier for example can air out any damp parts of your home.

. . .

If your open house is on a Saturday, don't cook a curry or even worse, a fish fry on the Friday night. Certain foods and spices can have a lingering smell. If you must, bake a loaf of bread in the morning, and certainly leave some cookies out if you're having an open house.

BEST FOODS FOR AN OPEN HOUSE

Surely the food you put out for an open house doesn't have that much of an effect? Think again.

Visuals, smells and tastes - you covered 3 senses there just by the food you're putting out. This ha a much larger psychological effect than you think.

Finger foods are the order of the day here. After all, you're not running a soup kitchen. You want something that looks nice on a table, people can take 1 or 2 without feeling a large commitment (who wants to eat a whole bowl of chili?) and ideally one or two items that fill the entire house with a warm scent to greet any buyer.

Don't go overboard on the spread either, you don't need to provide a full buffet for the entire neighborhood.

. . .

Placement of the food

If it's nice out, lay the food out on the patio or deck outside. That way they have to go through the house (and especailly the kitchen) to get it. This also deters noisy neighbors and free-food types (think Jason Seigel's character in *I Love You, Man*)

Chocolate Chip Cookies

The undisputed King of open house foods. They fill your kitchen with an irresistible scent that no mere mortal can resist. Everyone loves cookies and it gives a very good "welcome to your new home" vibe.

Lemonade

Summer and lemonade, is there a better combination?

Note, if it's winter, maybe re-think the lemonade and opt for hot chocolate instead. Remeber, houses don't always sell better in the summer!

Water

This one is obvious but having a case of water out is useful, especially if the weather is hot. This is beneficial is buyers come with kids as well, minimizing any child-based disruption is your key to a smooth open house.

Veggies and dip

It's like chips and dip without the crumbs. Plus the color variety adds an extra touch of glamor to the area.

. . .

Miniature Wrapped Candies

Easy, no clean up required, and like cookies they're irresistible to take 1 or 2. If you're absolutely on a budget - just put a bowl of these out and you're good to go.

RENOVATIONS THAT DECREASE THE VALUE OF YOUR HOME

THE ECONOMICS OF "ADDING VALUE"

One of the most confusing areas when doing major renovations, is that people focus far too much on a dollar figure or percentage increase in value when examining what area to improve.

For example, during the research phase of this book, I came across multiple websites that listed adding an additional bathroom as one of the best home improvements you could make. These sites cited data that the extra bathroom could increase the value of your home up to 10%.

What they don't take into account is the cost of implementing these new rooms, which at the mid-range level can often be more than double the amount you receive in return. For example if you have a $250,000 home, and you add a bathroom to attempt to increase the value by $25,000 - what you don't know is the new bathroom is going to cost a minimum of $40,000 to install, and often a lot more. With an ROI of less than 60%, these aren't a good investment at all if you're looking at sell.

Adding an extra bathroom - the numbers

Based on the latest 2017 survey from Remodelling Magazine, adding an extra bathroom costs an average of whopping $43,232 and yet only has an ROI of 53.9%.

Tired of waiting for your wife (or husband) to get out of the shower? Simply add a new one! Not so fast if you want to get a decent return on investment. Studies show that this is statistically the worst investment you can make in terms of home improvement.

Even luxury bathrooms, costing an average of just over $70,000 - only represented a slightly better ROI of 55%. So not even your jacuzzi or rain shower can save you from losing money. Whirlpool baths especially are seen as one of the worst and most unnecessary waste of square footage, so even one of these in your master bathroom is not a good investment if you plan on selling your home anytime soon.

For higher ROI on bathroom related fixes, replace the tiles. It's simple, pretty boring, and won't win you any design plaudits, but it is something that potential buyers will appreciate.

Making a giant master bedroom.

One of the biggest myths is that everyone wants a giant

master bedroom. More people are concerned with having more bedrooms, even if they don't currently have the family to use them. Many buyers think ahead while buying a house, and space for future family members plans heavily into this.

The same goes with removing closet space to extend the master bathroom, everyone needs closet space - but not everyone needs a huge bathroom. It's a matter of making your home appeal to the biggest possible market

Invisible improvements
Peaceful living may require a brand new plumbing system and HVAC (Heating, Ventilation and Air Conditioning) unit, but home buying is still very much a visual experience. Potential buyers are going to be far more enthused by a clean kitchen with sparkling countertops (even if they're 15 years old) than by a blanket statement of "we replaced the wiring last year." Home buyers often just expect the behind-the-scenes stuff like wiring and plumbing to be in full working order, and aren't willing to pay a premium just because you did it recently.

Visible and cosmetic improvements are what make buyers emotionally attached to a property, and emotional attachment is the reason people overpay for things. After all, when was the last time someone was "enamored" by brand new wiring?

Remodelling your home office
Despite the rise in working from home, and desktop entrepreneurs - not everyone wants a dedicated office space

in their home. In an age where square footage matters more than anything, a large home office is seen as wasteful. So before you go tearing down any walls, consider that the space could be much better put to use by adding another bedroom.

An external generator

Unless you live in a state where power outages are frequent, many buyers see this as wasteful, especially the frugal ones who are constantly worried about their utility bills. While you may see a handy backup solution, others see additional maintenance costs for something that may not even use once a year.

Trying to outgrow your area

Let's face it, no one wants a $400,000 home in a street surrounded by $250,000 homes. For one it draws extra attention to you and could well be a security risk. Secondly, buyers judge the quality of the neighborhood just as much as the quality of the house. Don't build an enormous extension, your money is better off spent elsewhere.

This also applies to the general standard of furnishing in your home. Think back to the consistency point made earlier in the book. If you have a top of the line, newly renovated $50,000 kitchen, but a bathroom that looks like it is stuck in a time warp from 1972 - this puts off potential buyers. You may see a beautiful kitchen, but they may see a $20,000 bathroom renovation project, that they neither have the time nor the money to worry about. If you have a large wad of cash burning a hole in your pocket and you have decided to make major renovations, it's better to evenly spread your money around than just focus on making one room stand out above the rest.

As a general guideline, your home value should not be anything more than 20% higher than the rest of your neighborhood, anything more than this can have an adverse effect.

IT'S TIME TO SELL

You've done the hard work, now it's time to reap your rewards with the sale. Check out these handy tips to put you on the right path.

GET THE RIGHT AGENT

Too often, people go for an agent through referral from a friend or family member. However, agents often specialize in certain price ranges or certain areas. If your agent did a great job on your sister-in-law's 2 bed apartment, she might not be the best choice for your 5 bed converted farmhouse.

Go to open houses in your area and your projected price range, get a feel for the agent and see if he or she is someone you'd want to work with. Open houses are as much a chance for agents to get new clients as they are for selling a house. Finding the right agent is vital and too often, money is left on the table by those who settle for the first agent they come across.

THE IMPORTANT OF TIMING

Timing your sale can often lead to up to a 20% increase in overall value. So if houses in your area aren't selling for the price you had in mind, it's worth it to hold off for a few months or even up to 2 years to get the figure you want. The other factor to note is what time of year you should list your house. Conventional wisdom has always said that spring and summer is the best time to sell - but that may not always be true. You see, because everyone knows this, there's a lot more competition during these months, and thus it may be harder for you to achieve your goal sale price.

Looking at the numbers, houses listed in winter (between December 21 and March 21) are more likely to sell within 6 months, spend 6 days less on the market and fetch a final sale price that's 1.2% *higher* than the equivalent home listed in any other season.

The reasoning for this is that serious home buyers will still be looking during the winter months, and these will be the ones more likely to make you the offer you want on your home.

REAL ESTATE AD TIPS

THINGS THAT YOU SHOULD MENTION IN YOUR AD

You may not think any of these matter when determining your home value, but they do. If any of these tick the boxes of your area, you should absolutely mention them to draw in niche buyers.

Proximity to sporting venues

Live a 15 minute drive away from MetLife stadium or just down the road from The American Airlines Arena? Write this down in your ad. Season ticket holders will go crazy for a location like this. One of the most annoying things about going to sports game is the potentially long drive to get there, so if you can show that the long drive no longer exists, or even better if you have public transit access, then you're onto a winner.

And non sporting fans? They won't really care, but it won't have a negative effect with them.

Proximity to Starbucks

Is there a Starbucks just down the street? People love the idea (even if they never go once they move in) of being able to sit outside with friends and family and enjoy a cup of their favorite caffeinated concoction. Starbucks also has a connotation with the area being affluent or "up and coming". So, if you have one near you, especially within walking distance - don't hesitate to let buyers or your realtor know.

Military Bases

Homes near army bases go for up to $50,000 more than the national median house price, and those near Navy, Marine and Coast Guard bases can be up to $90,000 more. Military members often don't have the luxury of being able to shop around when being assigned to a new base, and as such will likely overpay for a house in a convenient location moreso than other buyers.

Marijuana

Regardless of your personal views, the marijuana industry is one of the fastest growing in the entire countries. If you live in a recreational state, that's Alaska, Colorado, Maine, Massachusetts, Nevada, Oregon and Washington, (plus California from January 2018) for those of you keeping tabs - then your home price could be significantly impacted by the industry. Entrepreneurs, medical tourists and those looking to work in the industry are flocking towards these areas.

9 SECRETS YOUR REALTOR WON'T TELL YOU

1. If you get a last minute call to view, let them.

It may seem counterintuitive to let someone view your non-pristine home, but it's worth it. Last minute viewers are impulsive types, they might take a quick look around your house and make you an offer right there and then.

1. Never turn away a lowball offer

You're more likely to get a positive response by negotiating with someone who's already made an offer on your place than you are with a new prospect. Maybe these prospects had poor information regarding prices in the area, or maybe they were just trying their luck (anyone who has done any form of negotiating has done this at least once in their life).

1. Going with the agent who promises you the highest selling price, especially if it's way higher than everyone else.

There are always one or two agents who try this. It's the exact opposite situation to the previous issue. All they're doing with this tactic is trying to win your business. If you go with them, despite knowing better, your house is guaranteed to sit on the market, unsold, for a lot longer.

As this number increases, people start to speculate just why the house has been on the market for so long. There *must* be something wrong with it, and any offers that do come in are certain to be lowball ones.

Real estate investor and coach Phil Pustejovsky calls this the "kiss of death" - on one property alone this can cost you tens of thousands of dollars, and if you're a full-time investor that can add up to over 6 figures if you continue to make bad deals.

1. You can negotiate commissions

If you and your buyer are a few thousand apart, approach both of your realtors and see if they'll both reduce their commissions in order to get the deal done. It won't work every time, but it's always worth a shot.

1. Ask about their history, especially their recent history

Even though an agent might have had their license for years, they're only worth what they've done lately. For example, a family friend with 20 years in the business might not have sold a house within the past 3 years. Always ask a prospective agent about their recent dealings.

1. Sellers should guide buyers through their home to give a personal touch to the process.

Absolutely not, if you are glued to the side of a prospect,

you make them uneasy and feel like they're intruding in *your* home, not viewing what could potentially be *their* home. It's probably best if you aren't there for a viewing, and especially for an open house.

1. You should bide your time when you receive an offer, because it gives you more negotiating leverage.

In sales, delay is decay. Mood swings happen, people sour on offers. You don't benefit from delaying the transaction. If the offer is too low, negotiate - but negotiate right away.

1. Eventually someone will offer the price you wanted

This ties in with point number 3. If you selected an agent who listed at the highest price, and your property sits on the market for more than 30, 60 or even 90 days - buyers will notice this. They question what's wrong with the home, and the only offers you do get will be the lowball ones.

1. You shouldn't hire an agent with lots of other clients because they'll be too busy to focus on selling your home

There's a reason they have a lot of clients, it's because they're good. It's the same reason why popular restaurants are always busy, and the best cosmetic surgeons have month-long wait lists. These realtors have top quality assistants to help them with things like research and scheduling, they just focus on getting the best results for their clients.

AND THE 1, UNDISPUTED TRUTH?

You need a realtor to get the best value for your home

There's no substitute for experience, and selling a home is not something you become an expert in overnight. Yes, you'll save on commissions, but what use is that if you sell for 10 or 15% below market value? A study by the National Association of Realtors found the the average For Sale by Owner (FSBO) home sold for $185,000, whereas the average realtor sold home sold for $245,000 - that's a difference of a huge **$60,000**!

So even when you take out the average 6% commission for the agent, you're still leaving almost $50,000 on the table if you elect to sell your home yourself. I don't know about you, but to me that's not exactly the smartest financial decision.

Sellers aren't always the best judges of value, especially if it's a home you've lived in for a long time. More often than not, you will end up netting more by selling your home through a realtor, even after their commission is taken out.

Thanks to the internet, it's never been easier to get the best realtor for your home, websites such as http://www.realtrends.com/ allow you to search in your area for the realtor who has got the best results for their clients in terms of homes sold by dollar amount.

Remember, even an average realtor sells 11 homes a year, with the top ones coming out at around 35 sales per year. Don't leave a big financial decision up to chance by trying to do it all on your own just to save a few thousand on commissions - it's not worth it

HOW TO NEGOTIATE YOUR HOME SALE LIKE A PRO

More often than not, buyers who get less than they wanted for their home, do so not because they didn't make the right renovations, but because they're poor negotiators. By taking the time to learn some basic (yet highly effective) negotiation techniques, you put yourself is a much better position.

1. Remove all emotion from the deal

This may be hard if it's a home that's been in your family for over a hundred years. But guess what, when it comes to crunch time, your buyer doesn't care. Think of this like a simple business transaction, like you're selling staplers or juice boxes.

Remeber this: Successful real estate investors make a lot of their money buying from emotional sellers.

1. Establish a backup plan

In the real estate industry, this is known as a BATNA (best alternative to a negotiated agreement). This is when you decide your plan If you can't reach your desired amount. Maybe it's to hold onto the house for another year, or to rent it out in the meantime - but having a plan like this means you are less likely to accept a number that was below your target.

1. Really consider your first offer

Your first offer is likely to be the best one, so the first offer you receive is a good gauge of the market in general. This doesn't mean you have to sell at that price, but is does suggest that they want your house, and are willing to do what it takes to get it.

1. Counter it at your list price

What separates the amateurs from the pros when it comes to negotiation is countering. Often a buyer's offer will be low enough that the seller counters with an offer at below the list price. This is done as people naturally want to appear friendly, amiable or willing to compromise. Unfortunately, all these does is cost you, the seller, money.

Some buyers will be surprised by this, and will walk way - but by doing this you also avoid timewasters who are just trying to look for a bargain.

1. Create a bidding war

Bidding wars are fantastic as it allows buyers to compete against each other and push up the selling price. The easiest way to do this is to not entertain any offers at an open house, or before a certain date. For example, you put your house on the market and decide to tell you agent to not receive any offers for the first week. Often times, you may only get one offer using this strategy, but the offer will be higher than if you had just accepted all offers at the beginning.

Note: Creating a bidding war is not the same as fabricating one. Never tell the buyer there's another offer if there isn't one - it's easy for them to find out and if they call you out on it, you've lost a sale, plus your reputation takes a hit.

1. Don't give the buyer any leverage

For example, if they ask why you're selling, simply say you decided to move to a bigger property. They don't need to know you're behind on mortgage payments, or are moving halfway across the country - both of which signal that you need to get the transaction done quickly and would be easy to lowball.

TIPS FOR BUYING A HOME - SO YOU MAXIMIZE PROFIT DOWN THE LINE

We've previously covered emotion in buying and selling, and how it can cost you a good deal. But this is no more true on when buying a home. This especially applies to your first home, but is still very much relevant to any home you buy within the first 10 years of your real estate journey.

Why the first 10 years? This is the period of time before you experience the benefits of long-term investing with things such as compound interest. Your overall cash flow is lower, and your margin for error is thinner. Top South Carolina real estate investor Chad Carson, a man who started his journey with just $1,000 in his pocket says

"Particularly, in your first 10 years, if you make mistakes of buying emotionally on your residence as opposed to buying in a very calculated manner by making your residence a house-hack or a live-and-flip, or just renting and investing that somewhere else, the magnitude of that mistake is huge 20 to 30 years from now.

"It's like $700,000, [or] a million-dollar difference, for somebody 20 to 30 years later who made the choice to make their first home a nice home, a great neighborhood, and being in the top high school as opposed to making a decision to treat your home like an investment or just rent. It's a major, major difference."

HOW TO BEAT THE COMPETITION WHEN BUYING YOUR DREAM HOME

Chances are, you won't be the *only* ones in a good home buying position after reading this book. If you find a good deal on the market, there will be competition, so you'll have to place yourself in a position where your offer is the one the seller goes with. Now obviously, you want to do that in a way that doesn't involve spending drastically more money, and suddenly making a good deal into a bad one. Here are a number of ways you can appear like the most desirable candidate to any seller.

1. Ensure your finances are a fortress of stability

Just being pre-approved for a mortgage doesn't cut it any more, that's entry level stuff. In the internet age, it's never been so easy to get a pre-approval letter, and sellers are getting smart to this. If you want to stand out, then work with a reliable local mortgage lender or endorsed local provider (ELP) and have them give you the seal of approval

1. Show them you're serious

If you haven't heard of earnest money before, now's the time to learn. Earnest money is an amount you pledge as a deposit to the buyer to show them your true intentions of buying the home. Often this will be 1-2% of the total purchase price, but you can higher if there is competition. This doesn't mean you pay more for the house, as the money will be applied to your down payment - but by offering this up front, it puts you a step ahead of the competition. This also

1. Add a personal touch to the process

Consider submitting your offer in the form of a handwritten letter. This old-timey trick can put the seller at ease, and make a business transaction into a less formal event. You'll still need to be competitive with your offer, but if it's down to you and another buyer - this little letter may well swing things in your favor.

HOW TO GET THE MOST MONEY FOR YOUR HOME - EVEN IF YOU HAVE A DEADLINE TO SELL BY

In an ideal world, home sales would be a stress-free, blissful process - but we don't live in an ideal world, we live in the real world. People get new jobs and have to move to a new city, or parents get sick and require 24/7 care. This speeds up the sale process from one that takes months to something you have to finish within weeks. Whatever the reason, there are very few situations that are more stressful than having to sell a home quickly. Luckily, there are a number of ways to get the most for your home in situations like this.

1. List use house using a conservative price estimate.

This isn't the time to shoot for the moon, listing you house on the lower end of the price spectrum is likely to encourage multiple offers.

1. Set a deadline for offers

Use the principle of scarcity to encourage offers as well. People always want what they can't have, so setting a deadline, even if it's just 1 or 2 weeks after the house goes on the market, can net you multiple offers if buyers think they only have a limited window to get in on the deal.

1. Don't indicate you need to sell quickly

Following on from point 2, even though there's a deadline, you don't need to give a reason for one. You may be panicking inside, but your buyer doesn't need to know that. It's vital you keep a cool head during the selling process, and this can be tough if you are selling for emotional reasons (e.g. a death in the family)

1. Hire a Professional Stager

If time is tight, and renovations are out of the questions - consider hiring a professional home stager. A report by the National Assocation of Realtors (NAR) showed that 81% of buyers felt that staging helped them imagine the property they were viewing as a future home. Staged home also sell quicker than non-staged ones, and in some states the difference is staggering. In Oregon for example, pre-staged homes sold a huge 7 times faster than non-staged ones and in California the rate was 5 times faster.

Staging costs vary from state-to-state, but the national median tends to run around $600. Your real estate agent will have staging contacts, so it's best to use them as a resource if your time is limited.

1. Put away your cellphone camera

The vast majority of buyers now do research online before viewing a home. Poor quality photos that don't truly show off your home are guaranteed to lose you money when it comes to crunch time. So as tempting as it may be to whip out your iPhone and start snapping away, leave it to a pro. You don't even have to hire a pro to do this, even just getting a friend with a keen interest in photography and a knowledge of angles and lighting is enough. Even taking pictures in the right time of day with a proper camera is infinitely better than running around the house with any old cellphone camera.

1. Be flexible about viewing times

If you have serious time constraints, then you need to maximize what little time you do have to show your property. I advise scheduling viewing at all times of the day, even traditionally non-appealing times like evenings. This will involve keeping your home extremely clean at all time, in the case of a short-notice viewing. Remember, when you have buyers looking around - give them space

If you have pets, any signs of them should not be apparent in the home. Paraphernalia like dog bowls or cat litter boxes should be cleared away, and if you can help it - don't give any signs that pets are in the home. This isn't because your viewers aren't animal lovers, or don't have pets of their own, but it'll help them envisions their dream home easier.

1. Do the extra promotion yourself

If you're constrained by time, you're going to have to get creative if you want to maximize your return. Don't just leave the marketing element up to your agent. Get on social media, tell family and friends about the house. You never know which friend-of-a-friend-of-a-friend needs a house just like yours. If you're part of a home owners association, send your listing to their email list and you can get your neighbors to help advertise for you.

1. Use an essential oil diffuser to give a great first impression

If you don't have time to bake cookies 4 times a day (and who does?) to get that freshly baked smell wafting through the home, you can use an essential oil diffuser to get the same effect. You can put one near the door with a neutral scent like lavender or rosemary to gives a great first impression when a potential buyer walks through the door. Consider setting some fresh flowers out as well, this is a powerful visual tool that puts buyers in the right mood as soon as they walk in your door.

8.5 Use a drop of vanilla in a warmed oven to replicate the smell of freshly baked cookies

An old realtor hack, if you don't have time to bake, just do the above and your house will smell like freshly baked cookies!

1. Avoid guaranteed sales programs

Have you ever seen those ads from realtors that say "If you don't sell your home within 30 days, we'll buy it". All these people do is list your home at a price no one is willing to pay, then give you a lowball offer at the end of the 30 day period. Causing you to take a massive loss.

1. List your home on a Thursday or Friday

Doing this will put your fresh in the minds of buyers and agents when they're planning their weekend viewings. A study by real estate website Redfin found that homes listed on a Friday sold for an average of $2,800 higher than homes listed on a Sunday.

UNTITLED

CONCLUSION

So, there we have it, cheap, creative ways, and even free ways that you can maximize the value of your home. Applying just a few of these to your home sale can net profits of 5, 10 or even 20% higher than you would have received without them.

Now compound those profits over multiple homes and we're potentially talking about hundreds of thousands of dollars - not bad for a few coats of paint, or a smart decision on which day of the week you list your home!

I hope you've learned a lot in this book and you can use the tips in your own home sale. Selling a home can be stressful, especially if this is your first go around the block, but when armed with what you've learned in this book, you can be confident about netting the highest possible sale price for you and your family.

REFERENCES

Imbert, F. & Francolla, G. (2018). *Facebook's $100 Billion-Plus Rout Is the Biggest Loss in Stock Market History.* Retrieved from https://www.cnbc.com/2018/07/26/facebook-on-pace-for-biggest-one-day-loss-in-value-for-any-company-sin.html

Kondo, M. (2016). Spark Joy: An Illustrated Master Class on the Art of Organizing and Tidying Up. Berkeley, CA: Ten Speed Press.

Miao, L. (2016). Guilty Pleasure or Pleasurable Guilt? Affective Experience of Impulse Buying in Hedonic-Driven Consumption. *Journal of Hospitality & Tourism Research 35*(1), 79-101, doi: 10.1177/1096348010384876

Moniuszko, S. (2019). *Lilly Singh, the First Openly Bisexual Woman of Color Talk Show Host, on Impact of Coming Out.* Retrieved from https://www.usatoday.com/story/entertainment/celebrities/2019/08/21/lilly-singh-talks-impact-her-coming-out-bisexual-india/2070921001/

Richardson, T. (2015). *The Science and Psychology of Debt and Mental Health* [PowerPoint slides]. Retrieved from School of Psychology, University of Southampton, Open Access &

Institutional Repository. Ruben, M. (2009). *Forgive Us Our Trespasses? The Rise of Consumer Debt in Modern America* [Report]. Retrieved from College of Information Sciences and Technology, Pennsylvania State University, Cite Seer X.

Rodriguez, M. *IHRSA 2018 Global Report: Health Club Industry Revenue Totaled $87.2 Billion in 2017.* Retrieved from

https://www.ihrsa.org/about/media-center/press-releases/ihrsa-2018-global-report-club-industry-revenue-totaled-87-2-billion-in-2017/

REFERENCES

Alonso, L., Rodriguez, C., & Rojo, R. (2015). From Consumerism to Guilt: Economic Crisis and Discourses about Consumption in Spain. *Journal of Consumer Culture 15*(1), 68-85, doi: 10.1177/1469540513493203

Alterman, L. (2019). *What Is a Tiny House? A Huge Trend Explained in Simple Terms.* Retrieved from https://www.realtor.com/advice/buy/what-is-a-tiny-house/

Amar, M., Ariely, D., Ayal, S., Cryder, C., & Rick, S. (2011). Winning the Battle but Losing the War: The Psychology of Debt Management. *Journal of Marketing Research, Forthcoming.* Retrieved from https://ssrn.com/abstract=1760528

Bauer, M., Wilkie, J., Kim, J., & Bodenhausen, G. (2012). Cuing Consumerism: Situational Materialism Undermines Personal and Social Well-Being. *Psychological Science 23*(5), 517-523, doi: 10.1177/0956797611429579

Baumgartner, S. (2019). *Lucy Hale and David Dobrik to Host 2019 Teen Choice Awards.* Retrieved from https://www.etonline.com/lucy-hale-and-david-dobrik-to-host-2019-teen-choice-awards-129478

Bridges, F. (2018). *Why You Should Limit Your Time on Social Media.* Retrieved from https://www.forbes.-

com/sites/francesbridges/2018/08/30/why-you-should-limit-your-time-on-social-media/#5065573e9146

Department of Numbers. (2017). *Us Household Income.* Retrieved from

https://www.deptofnumbers.com/income/us/

Experian. (2019). *A Look at U.S. Consumer Credit Card Debt.* Retrieved from https://www.experian.com/blogs/ask-experian/state-of-credit-cards/

Harari, D. (2018). *Household Debt: Statistics and Impact on Economy.* United Kingdom: House of Commons Library.

Heeb, G. (2019). *American household debt just hit a new record high.* Retrieved from https://markets.businessinsider.com/news/stocks/us-household-debt-just-climbed-to-fresh-highs-2019-2-1027947029

www.ingramcontent.com/pod-product-compliance
Lightning Source LLC
Chambersburg PA
CBHW050000230526
45465CB00003BB/1188